KW-363-244

On the Road to Democracy

The Czech Republic from Communism To Free Society

Václav Klaus

President of the Czech Republic

Editor
Dr. John C. Goodman

Project Manager
Wess Mitchell

Cover photo:
Václav Klaus speaks to the National Center for Policy Analysis Chairman's Club Conference at Prague Castle, October 2003.

The NCPA Distinguished Leader Award and the publication of this book were made possible by The Charlotte and Walter Kohler Charitable Trust.

Available from the National Center for Policy Analysis,
12770 Coit Rd., Suite 800, Dallas, Texas 75251
Telephone: 972-386-6272

www.ncpa.org

ISBN 1-56808-143-X

©2005 by the National Center for Policy Analysis, Dallas, Texas. All rights reserved. No part of this publication may be used or reproduced in any manner whatsoever without permission in writing from the National Center for Policy Analysis except in the case of brief quotations embodied in news articles, critical articles, or reviews. The views expressed in the publications of the National Center for Policy Analysis are those of the authors and do not necessarily reflect the views of the staff, officers, or board members of the NCPA.

Table of Contents

Foreword

The Mont Pelerin Society is an international organization founded by Friedrich Hayek in 1947 with now about 600 members from many nations that aims through discussion of ideas to promote economic, political and social freedom. In 1991, the Society chose Prague as the location of its first meeting behind the former Iron Curtain. The desire to meet so soon in the former Soviet communist empire is not surprising, but Prague was chosen not simply because of its beauty and central location. The main reason was their dynamic and strong free market oriented Finance Minister, Václav Klaus, who very much wanted to host this Meeting because of his admiration for many members of the Society, and as evidence of Czechoslovakia's commitment to freedom.

I was then president of the Society, and was involved in planning the program, and in contact with the local organizers. Not surprisingly, the theme of this meeting was the transition out of communism. Klaus and a small group of committed market-oriented economists around him privatized with a bang through a rapid, thorough and innovative system based on providing the population with ownership vouchers in former state enterprises. Several of these economists, including Klaus, were on the program and participated actively in the meeting. They discussed the mechanics of their privatization program, and other challenges and plans for their transition toward a free market economy.

I got to know Václav Klaus some at this meeting, and was impressed of course by the revolution he was leading in Czechoslovakia. In addition, I admired how he had managed to think deeply about economic problems during the very trying prior couple of decades when he had limited access to economic writings, and was prevented from attending professional meetings in other countries. We spoke about the ideas of Hayek, Friedman, Stigler and other leading free market economists, many associated with the Chicago School of Economics. Over the years, our friendship ripened as we met at other Mont Pelerin meetings — he was the first person elected to the Society from a formerly communist nation; through a couple of additional trips I made to Prague [in *Gary Becker in Prague* (Prague, 1996) we engaged in a "debate" on public policies], and in several visits he made to the University of Chicago.

After being Finance Minister for several years, Klaus became prime minister, then head of parliament, and is now president of the Czech Republic. In a decade, the economy of this Republic has become mainly private, whereas it was virtually 100 per cent state-run when they started. Czechoslovakia in the meantime split into two independent, although friendly nations, and both are doing well — which shows that small nations can prosper in a global economy.

Both the Czech Republic and Slovakia have been admitted to the European Union, and they are subject to the growing bureaucracy of that Union, as well as benefiting from belonging to a large open market in people, capital and goods. Václav Klaus has not been an enthusiastic advocate of joining the EU — see his essay in this collection, "The Czech Republic and the EU: a Marriage of Convenience, Not of Love" — although he recognizes the political advantages and some economic benefits along with the significant costs.

This book collects some of his lectures during the past 12 years on various themes related to the transition out of communism, integration into Europe and world developments. They reveal original and courageous thinking about how best to manage a never-before attempted rapid transition from a centrally planned to a decentralized economy. Economists in the United States and elsewhere offered few guidelines and vast disagreements about how best to do this. He readily admits that some mistakes were made along this unknown path, and he emphasizes that expectations often greatly exceeded possibilities. Still, it is truly impressive how much was achieved in such little time.

I find the vast majority of his arguments persuasive and well reasoned, although I do not agree that the United States should not have gone into Iraq, and I have a few other disagreements. But overall this is a remarkable collection of essays written during arguably the most remarkable decade of the 20th century, when communism fell throughout the Soviet Empire, and was replaced by free and market-oriented nations. Klaus was both a leading thinker about this transformation and one of the most influential practitioners. This combination of theory and practice gives him unique insights that are on dazzling display in this collection. When combined with an excellent English writing style, the temptation to read, ponder and benefit is irresistible.

Gary S. Becker

University of Chicago

Introduction

On November 17, 2004, the people of the Czech Republic celebrated 15 years of independence from communist rule. For the millions of Czechs who are old enough to remember what life was like behind the Iron Curtain, the contrast with their country today could not be more profound. For four decades, Czechs were virtual slaves within their own borders. They were told what they could and could not read, when and where they could assemble, how much they could buy and sell, and even what they could and could not say. They worked in state-owned factories, read state-owned newspapers, drove cars from state-owned companies, and ate food from state-owned farms.

The result was a country whose economy and society were much poorer than those of Western European countries. Today's Czech economy is one of the most vibrant in Europe, with per capita income near $16,000 and a gross domestic product of $161 billion. Czechs are not only wealthier than ever before, they are also freer. Residents of Prague now can choose from more than a dozen newspapers. They can choose from an unlimited number of political parties — five of them are now in the parliament — compared to practically only one under communism. They can buy products from all over the world and sell them all over the world. They can travel to neighboring countries, form their own businesses, criticize the government, and assemble in city squares without fear of reprisal from government tanks.

For the Czech people, the past 15 years have been, to modify Nobel laureate Frederich Hayek's famous phrase, the road out of serfdom. Unlike the road that led them in, the way out was not planned. There was no instruction manual, no central planning committee, no roadmap to a new state. No one had ever dismantled a communist government before and built a new one from scratch in its place. But in Czechoslovakia — as in other Central and Eastern European countries — there were small groups of individuals who came forward to lead the way out. These were the founding fathers of the post-communist era, and many of them were unlikely leaders. In East Germany, a musician became president. In Poland, a journalist was elected prime minister. In Czechoslovakia, the new leader — Václav Havel — was a playwright.

And then there was an economist. When the communist government collapsed in November 1989, Václav Klaus was a researcher working at the Forecasting Institute of the Czechoslovak Academy of Sciences. Like Havel, Klaus was known for his subversive attitude toward the socialist system. But unlike Havel or any of the other leaders from artistic or journalistic backgrounds, Klaus had been trained as an economist and in the more liberal era of the '60s studied even in Italy and the United States (Cornell University). He was the least likely of dissidents. His education was the best the system could provide: a degree in the Economics of Foreign Trade from the Prague School of Economics and a Ph.D. at the Institute of Economics of the Czechoslovak Academy of Sciences. He discovered the great free market writers – Frederich Hayek, Ludwig von Mises, Milton Friedman - and his research converted him to free market thinking.

Klaus was most impressed by Hayek. His first encounter with Hayek came in the summer of 1968, when he attended a conference in Austria where Hayek was a guest speaker. The event had a strong impact on Klaus — not so much because of what Hayek said, but because of its timing. On the third day of the conference, just before Hayek was scheduled to speak, the Soviet Union and other Warsaw Pact armies invaded Czechoslovakia. When Klaus returned home to Prague, the city was occupied by Russian tanks. Klaus was — due to his views — fired from the Academy of Sciences and spent the next 16 years working for the State Bank of Czechoslovakia. His experience provided a clear contrast between the competing free market and communist systems. In one, individuals are free to pursue their own goals, without interference from the state. In the other, the state imposes its goals on individuals — if necessary, by force.

For Klaus, there was never much doubt about which of these was the surest way to provide for human wants and secure individual happiness. Like so many other Czechs of his generation, Klaus recoiled at the communist state's heavy-handed methods, and knew that such a system could never succeed in winning the hearts and minds of the people. But as an economist, his understanding of the problem went much deeper. Whereas other Czech intellectuals objected mainly to the use of force while retaining their faith in socialist ideology, Klaus realized early on that the system itself was the problem. Where others looked for ways to reform socialism at the margin, Klaus understood from his reading of Hayek that the only way forward was to uproot the entire system and replace it with capitalism. Like Hayek, Klaus understood that even the milder forms of state intervention are doomed to failure.

Reaching this conclusion went against the grain of Klaus' training. Like other students from the communist education system, Klaus had been taught that the more complex a society becomes, the more government is needed to manage it. But in reading Hayek, Klaus came to recognize an inverse relationship between the level of complexity in society and the ability of the state to effectively regulate human affairs.

Becoming Hayek's disciple did not help Klaus' career. For years, he was relegated to marginalized posts in the government bureaucracy. In the fall of 1989, there was every reason to believe that he would remain in these posts forever, and live out the remainder of his life in obscurity. But when the system began to fall apart and the country finally showed that it was ready for the types of reform that Hayek had advocated, Klaus found himself catapulted into the national spotlight. He was one of the few men around who seemed to have a coherent understanding of what needed to be done next. The speed of his ascent in the years that followed is a testament to his capabilities as a politician, reformer and economist. He was one of the founding fathers of the Civic Forum (a leading political organization) and later its chairman. Three weeks after the Velvet Revolution he became Finance Minister. In the spring of 1991, he founded the Civic Democratic party (which is the counterpart of U.S. Republican party) and was its chairman for 11 years. In 1992 he became Prime Minister. Then in 2003 — just 14 years after leaving his job as a researcher — Václav Klaus became President of the Czech Republic.

By any measure, Klaus' political career has been one of superlatives. He led the longest-lived post Soviet reform government and presided over the peaceful separation of Czechoslovakia into two new states — Slovakia and the Czech Republic. Between 1989 and 1996, his policies brought about a period of economic growth known as the "Czech Miracle." In 1989, only three percent of Czech GDP was in the private sector. Under Klaus' steady hand, the country discarded its massive government structure and quickly outstripped many Eastern, as well as Western, European countries. By the end of his term, the country had repaid loans from the International Monetary Fund two years ahead of schedule, gained admission to the OECD, and earned an "A" rating from Standard & Poor's. Perhaps most tellingly, Klaus' economic reforms were embraced by his successors, the social democrats. The country now has one of the highest per capita incomes in Central Europe, and attracts $5 billion annually in foreign investment. Among former Soviet satellites, the Czech Republic is the only country where communists have not returned to power in the national legislature.

Václav Klaus has been called many things: "the Milton Friedman of Czechoslovakia," "the Margaret Thatcher of Eastern Europe." And while the ranks of Eastern Europe's post-communist reform leaders are filled with larger-than-life luminaries — Havel, Lech Walesa, Viktor Orban — it is no exaggeration to say that Klaus fits into his own separate category. What sets Klaus apart from other European leaders, and what makes his career one that is worth studying, is his proven ability to combine the professions of economist and politician. Throughout his political career, Klaus has always managed to keep one foot in the world of ideas. He is equally at home in a cabinet meeting or presenting a paper at an academic conference. Unlike most of the leaders who have taken office since the fall of communism, Klaus has a deep understanding of economic theory, and has allowed free market principles to shape his policies.

This book presents a long overdue restatement of Klaus' challenge to the socialist model and shows that his ideas are as relevant today in the struggle against the expansionary welfare state as they were in the struggle against communism. It consists of 45 of Klaus' most memorable speeches and lectures, organized into four chapters — two of which look back at the lessons learned in the period after communism and two of which look forward to future challenges and opportunities.

In the first chapter, "The Challenges of the Post-Communist Era," Klaus looks back on the years immediately following the fall of the Iron Curtain, what went wrong, and what went right. As he predicted in 1989, the transition from communism to a free society proved not to be a frictionless process. A gap emerged between what people expected and what democracy and free markets delivered. This gap — which Klaus calls the "expectations-reality gap" — has widened with time, leading many Eastern Europeans to look back to the state for solutions.

In the second chapter, "The Economics of Transition," Klaus shows how the transition to capitalism involved two parallel processes: economic liberalization (deregulation, privatization, etc.) and the development of the political and legal institutions necessary for markets to function efficiently. As it turned out, liberalization was achieved almost instantly, but building an institutional infrastructure is a lengthy process that takes time — decades, in fact. As with the expectations-reality gap, the gap between markets and institutions has led many of Klaus' countrymen to reminisce about the certainties of the communist era.

In the third chapter, "Europe and Its Integration," Klaus turns his attention to the European Union (EU), which some see as a solution to the problems that have emerged in the transition to capitalism. At the heart of the EU project is a desire to find a so-called "Third Way" between capitalism and socialism by mingling elements of free enterprise and government planning. This is something that Hayek warned against for decades and that threatens to re-introduce many of the socialist policies that Klaus fought so hard to dismantle. However, rather than taking a "euro-skeptical" approach, Klaus argues that Eastern Europeans should pursue a course of "euro-realism" — closely guarding national sovereignty and working within the EU to promote free market alternatives to collectivist thinking.

In the fourth and final chapter, "Reflections on the World," Klaus considers the challenges and opportunities of the new century. Contrary to what many scholars believe, he argues that the end of communism did not bring an end to the great ideological debates of the 20th century. Antiliberal ideas persist in the form of "third way" economic thinking, radical environmentalism, and various other communitarian ideologies. According to Klaus, the Western traditions of individual freedom, democracy, and open markets must be vigorously promoted and protected from these new ideologies if they are to be kept alive for future generations.

John C. Goodman

President

National Center for Policy Analysis

Chapter 1:

THE CHALLENGES OF THE POST-COMMUNIST ERA

Václav Klaus and former Prime Minister Margaret Thatcher at the Churchill Memorial in Winston Churchill Square, Prague, November 1999.

Transforming Toward a Free Society

1996 Walter Wriston Lecture for the Manhattan Institute for Policy Research, New York, September 26, 1996

Thank you for inviting me to come here and for giving me the opportunity to share with you some of my ideas about my country, about the post-communist world, and, implicitly, about Europe and your country as well. I will of course use my experience, both from the communist era and from the transition years, as my main perspective.

Almost seven years after the so-called Velvet Revolution, the Czech Republic has completed its basic transformation from a communist society to a free society based on a pluralistic political system and a free market economy. The relative success of the transformation process was made possible by:

- a clear vision of the society we wanted to establish;
- the ability of political leaders who were suddenly and unexpectedly put into their positions after the collapse of communism to prepare and implement a pragmatic and realizable transformation strategy;
- the ability of political leaders to gather sufficient public support for the measures, which were often painful and therefore not popular.

The easiest part of the whole process was the *political transformation*. It was put in place through a simple and rapid liberalization step: the introduction of free entry into the political market. As a result, new political entities started to emerge almost overnight. They started to formulate their political programs and to establish their local branches throughout the whole country. They began their fierce and, in principle, healthy political infightings. Nothing else was necessary. What followed naturally was a pure, spontaneous evolution. After the initial extreme atomization of the political spectrum (with more than 100 political parties or quasi-parties at one point), the more or less standard spectrum of political parties with clearly defined ideological positions has gradually been created. To a large extent the current political structure of the Czech Republic resembles those found in Western Europe. This new structure led to coalition governments and, in spite of the relative weakening of the ruling coalition in the recent parliamentary elections, the Czech government remains as the only right-of-center government of the post-communist world.

The *social transformation* took longer. It started with the abolition of the most visible aspects of the communist paternalistic system, subsidized food prices. It continued with the radical liberalization of prices, which had been fixed for 40 years under communist control. Only a few prices still remain regulated (rents, prices of electric energy). Deregulation continues according to a pre-announced annual formula so that we expect to reach the equilibrium level of nearly all prices in the near future. An important step forward was the fundamental reform of the social transfer system with the introduction of means-tested social benefits last year. One might feel that the system is still too generous; but we envisage further adjustments in the future.

The overall climate within the society has changed. Individual responsibility, rather than waiting for help, is becoming the dominant social philosophy and psychology. We do not underestimate the role which social policy — organized by the state — should play in a healthy society. However, we do not share the currently prevailing European concept of a social market economy with an overextended welfare-state philosophy.

In the *economic sphere*, we have been consistently trying to follow basic, well-known, conservative axioms. We have insisted on healthy finance and on a balanced budget, which we have had for seven consecutive years. Also, we have insisted on continuous reductions in the state budget's share of gross domestic product (GDP), on vigorous deregulation and liberalization and on rapid mass privatization of what used to be the state-owned economy.

We understood that the role of privatization is absolutely crucial. One qualification was, however, necessary. The task was to find new private owners, rather than to maximize the government's proceeds from privatization. I have to admit that we had trouble explaining this to our Western partners and friends. To privatize as quickly as possible, we could not rely completely on standard privatization methods, which are useful when a government privatizes marginal parts of a whole economy. We fashioned our own program, so-called voucher privatization. This procedure made it possible to privatize quickly and on a large scale with the involvement of millions of our citizens. This rapid privatization, which led to a situation where the private sector produces three-quarters of GDP today (it was zero in 1989), proved to be the catalyst for the whole process. Today, we face no additional radical, far-reaching measures in the economic field. Now the maturing of the whole system will depend more and more on the spontaneous evolution of all the micro-agents involved and less on the government's policies.

In the *international sphere* we have changed our previous "Eastern orientation." Organizations such as the Warsaw Pact and COMECON were dissolved and our present aim is to become full members of the European Union and NATO. However, this does not imply that we do not wish to continue our cooperation with the countries on other continents as well as with the countries of the former communist bloc. This can be demonstrated by the fact that the Czech Republic is a founder and a very active member of CEFTA, the Central European Free Trade Area, which has become a very fruitful integration endeavor.

To discuss all of these developments in more detail would not be very interesting to this audience. Therefore, I wish to continue by discussing deeper, more general aspects. When speaking recently at an international meeting in Vienna, I was asked what the tricks are, how it was achieved. I would like to make an attempt to say a few words about that now.

The transformation of the whole society is an *evolutionary process* which is composed of a very complicated mixture of planned and unplanned movements, of intended and unintended events, a process which is based on a rather delicate mixture of intentions and spontaneity — to use the famous Hayekian terminology. This interpretation of events — however simple and trivial — proved to be very useful for both the theoretical discussions and the practical policy-making. It was an approach disliked only by those who had immodest ambitions of social engineering and who — after the collapse of communism — tried to make use of a unique opportunity to construct such a complex phenomenon as a new social system, and to fine-tune its emergence. Some of us have been warning against all kinds of left-wing social constructivism but I am afraid that a few years ago even some of us tended to make a similar mistake. We should know that capitalism cannot be "introduced." We should know that it must evolve, grow, gain strength and mature in the way described so clearly by Hayek.

In discussing the transformation from communism (not from an interventionist welfare state), I suggest starting with the nontrivial idea that the communist system collapsed, that it was not defeated. It collapsed because it was in an advanced stage of decomposition, because it gradually lost its two strongest constitutive elements — *the fear* on one hand and *the faith* on the other. In its final days, the communist system became both soft and unconvincing, and such a state of affairs could not continue. It is an irony of history that communism — sort of — melted down, which is something that some of our brave colleagues in the post-communist world do not like to be reminded of. Part of their aura would be lost and that is the reason why they try to contest such an interpretation of events. But I am convinced that it is correct.

We are being confronted with the idea that the collapse of communism created a vacuum. At first sight this seems plausible, but it is not. What remained was not a vacuum. We inherited weak and, therefore, inefficient markets and a weak, inefficient democracy. Both the economic and political mechanisms were shallow, the political and economic agents were new, weak and fragile and the outcomes of their interplay were, therefore, less efficient than in a fully grown free society as you know it from the countries which have never experienced communism and where the spontaneous, evolutionary (Hayekian) process of institution-building and agent-formation has never been interrupted. In spite of that, there was no need (not to speak about the possibility) to fill the newly created space with a ready-made, imported-from-outside, delivered system. We had to move at the margin and make incremental changes. No masterminding of the evolution of a free society was possible.

On the other hand, I agree with those who make the point that it was not possible to wait for a sufficient degree of market efficiency. The quick abolition of old institutions was a *sine qua non* for success because it was the only way to minimize the non-negligible transition costs. At the beginning the weak markets were no more efficient than the command economy which existed before, but this should not become an argument against early liberalization and deregulation measures.

The relative weakness or strength of institutions of a newly formed free society is only one aspect of the whole issue. What about the people? Are they ready for such a rapid change? Does free society presuppose — in addition to the creation of its basic institutions — some set of values or moral standards that would properly anchor the society? Do the people need an interim period of "schooling?" Is such schooling realizable? Are there teachers for such a procedure? Are the people willing to be educated? My answer to these and similar questions is simple. The people are always ready and they do not need a special education. What they need is a free space for their voluntary activities, the elimination of controls and prohibitions of all kinds.

When I speak about a free society, what kind of free society do I have in mind? Should we transform ourselves toward a theoretical model of free society or toward a real free society as we see it in many forms in Western Europe and

North America? Theoretically, the answer is simple and straightforward. The closer we get to the ideal case, the better. In reality, it is more complicated. Whenever I try at home to avoid introducing an illiberal piece of legislation or to repeal an existing one, I am reminded of the same law in one Western country or another, or — recently more and more often — I am being told that what I do not want to accept is the recent recommendation or instruction of the European Commission. Following such examples can become — paradoxically — a constraint on our spontaneous evolution toward a "free society."

After the collapse of "hard" communism, we rejected reformed communism, we avoided romantic nationalism (with its very negative systemic consequences), we overcame utopian attempts to forget everything and to start building a brave new world based on aprioristic, moralistic and elitist ambitions (of those who are better than the rest of us). But our remaining task is not to end up with the kind of statist, interventionist, paternalistic social-democratism that we see in so many free societies to the west of us.

We know that it is our task to attack the expanding state, which was — and still is — a dominant tendency of the 20th century, of the century of socialisms with a variety of confusing adjectives. The majority of intellectuals and social scientists of this century considered this tendency to be almost an iron law of history. We have to demonstrate that it is possible to return to the liberal (in the European sense) social order.

The Transformation of Czech Society: Retrospect and Prospect

The 1997 Annual Hayek Memorial Lecture, Institute of Economic Affairs, London, June 17, 1997

It is a great honor and a great pleasure for me to be here at the Institute of Economic Affairs and to be invited to deliver a lecture connected with the name of Friedrich von Hayek, a man from whom I have learned so much. The fact that the Sixth Annual Hayek Memorial Lecture is held today reminds us that it is six years since we have lost one of the greatest men of this century. Let me begin with several personal remarks.

The day before the Velvet Revolution in my country in November 1989 I was — after more than 20 years — in Austria, at the University of Linz. I met the members of the economics department in the afternoon and in the evening I participated in a panel discussion about reforms in the communist countries. To my great surprise, I was told that neither Hayek nor the Austrian School of Economics was included in the obligatory reading list for students at the university. The night before the famous student demonstration in Prague, which triggered the whole change, I assured the overcrowded hall that if the Austrian school of economics had gone dead in Austria, we would keep it alive in Prague. It was a daring statement at that time. The audience reacted with long-lasting applause, and I have to admit that I did not know then just how soon we would have a chance to start realizing this promise.

I mentioned visiting Austria after a very long period of time. I had a unique opportunity to see Hayek when visiting Austria 21 years before that. But it was at the most curious moment. In August 1968 I took part in a well-known international conference organized in a beautiful Austrian Alpine resort called Alpbach. I was truly looking forward to it because the organizers invited very interesting speakers, including Friedrich von Hayek. The third day of this conference was August 21, 1968, the day of the Soviet invasion of Czechoslovakia and, as it happened, Hayek's speech was held the afternoon after the invasion. I nevertheless came to the conference auditorium, but I just came to see him as I was not able to pay any attention to the words he was saying.

There is no doubt that Hayek was extremely important — for us in the former communist countries, but I am sure for you as well — both for his comprehensive criticism of communist society and economy as well as for his radical and very deep criticism of all softer forms of socialism and interventionism. He was also important for giving us guidance on how to build a free society and market economy and for helping steer you in the West away from the slippery road which inevitably leads to socialism.

I myself discovered Hayek in the second half of the '60s, during the well-known Czechoslovak economic reform era. It was a period full of attempts to reform something which was in principle unreformable, to combine "plan and market," or — to put it differently — to use the market as an instrument in the experienced and omnipotent hands of the planners. My country at that time was at the forefront of such reforms and we (or at least some of us) came across the famous "socialist controversy" which pitted Austrians Mises and Hayek on one side against neoclassical economists Lange and Lerner on the other. I was fully (and maybe even partly subconsciously) on the side of the Austrians. I knew that markets must be real, not fictitious or artificial, that we cannot "play the market," that the players of the game must be economic agents, using their own, very real money, not symbols. I even translated excerpts of this controversy into Czech and published them in a widely read literary monthly. I became a true Hayekian for the rest of my life.

Intellectually, the most important and most relevant of Hayek's contributions — at least for us at that time — was his well-known "Use of Knowledge in Society," which was published in the *American Economic Review* in 1945.

Hayek's article explained very clearly and persuasively that relevant economic information can never be transmitted to the planning center because of the very nature of information (not because of the absence or insufficiency of information technology) and that planning is applicable only in a simple economy, whereas a complex economy needs the market. This counterintuitive idea was absolutely crucial. He succeeded in fully reversing the socialist or social democratic argument of this century, which held that the more complex society gets, the more we need government. Instead, he said that the more complex society becomes, the less competent governments become in regulating it.

You may be surprised that I have not mentioned *The Road to Serfdom*. The reason is very simple. I did not know the book at that time. In a communist country, it was always easy to get the last copy of the *American Economic Review* or of the *Economic Journal* but very difficult to get a political or ideological pamphlet. I read *The Road to Serfdom* much later than the main scientific contributions of Hayek.

The second most important of Hayek's contributions for me was his criticism of constructivism, of social engineering, of immodest ambitions of intellectuals to set up an ideal social order. His works "The Results of Human Action but not of Human Design," "The Intellectuals and Socialism," "Counter-Revolution of Science," "Scientism and the Study of Society" and "The Pretence of Knowledge" (to name just some of them) helped us understand the basis of society and the logic of its spontaneous evolution.

This theoretical idea was no less important for the formation of a free society and market economy after the collapse of communism. It is connected with our experience that the fundamental transformation of a country is necessarily a complicated and fragile mixture of intentions on the side of politicians (and reformers) and spontaneity of human behavior on the side of millions of free citizens, a mixture of revolution and evolution, a mixture of continuity and discontinuity, a mixture of successes and failures, a mixture of widely applauded measures and of moves that are neither welcomed nor appreciated.

We in the Czech Republic are continuously in and out of the past. On one hand, we are positively surprised at how far and how fast we have already moved compared to more than 40 years of communism, but on the other hand, we are (or some of our fellow-citizens are) disappointed that life at home has not yet reached the smoothness and easiness of life here in London where — if I am not wrong — the last episode of totalitarianism was hundreds of years ago. There have been many simplified and misleading propositions about the dismantling of communism and the formation of a free society and a market economy. And as usual, there were optimists and pessimists among us. The first group underestimated the heritage of communism and overestimated the human ability to mastermind such a complex task. The second group underestimated the strength of the spontaneous activity of human beings when they are really free. I would argue that we were neither unconstrained optimists nor pessimists waiting for help from outside.

Hayek would give us a straightforward suggestion. Do not try to mastermind the systemic evolution. Do not intervene into microeconomic decision-making. Do not try to accelerate economic growth by means of expansionary, Keynesian-style fiscal and monetary policies at the macro level. He would advise us to continue deregulation, liberalization and privatization. To take care of rules, not of outcomes. To take a long-term, not short-term position. To believe in impersonal social mechanisms, not in elitist engineering of social phenomena.

We are aware of such recommendations. We will follow them, but I hope they will be taken seriously outside the post-communist world as well. I have in mind Europe in general and this country in particular.

Systemic Transformation and Its Costs

University of Arizona, Tucson, November 13, 1997

I am extremely pleased and really honored by being awarded the Honorary Doctorate Degree at your university. I am aware of the distinguished list of predecessors who have achieved this recognition and I thank you for including me in this group. I take it as a personal award but, at the same time, I know that it is a form of recognition of my country's achievements in the last several years after the breakdown of communism and of my modest role in this unrepeatable and therefore difficult transformation process, in the transition from communism to a free society.

I am not able to appreciate or evaluate the role of the University of Arizona in the academic life of your country, but looking at it from a distance, looking at it from Prague, from the Czech Republic, from a former communist country, from a country which has been undergoing in the last eight years the most radical transition to a free society and market economy, this university is connected with the name of Gordon Tullock and his contribution to the public choice school of economic science.

Let me use — at least partly — this perspective for my short address today. I know that the public choice school was originally created for the analysis of the behavior and decision-making of the government and other public authorities in a standard Western society, but I can assure you that we — in the communist era — understood immediately that it was even more relevant to the analysis of our own, very statist, very "public" and very quasi-collectivistic system where the role of the government is both nominally and really much bigger than even in the most interventionist capitalist country. The irrationalities of the reliance on "public choice" were more visible than in your country.

We knew from our own experience that there is nothing like a genuine "public interest" and especially that there is nobody who could represent it. We saw concrete individuals hidden behind the so called "public interest" and we saw the partiality of those interests pushed forward by various individuals or regional or professional groupings. They had no connection with or justification for anything that can be considered "public interest." In the dark communist days it was almost a revelation and definitely an enormous help to come across the ideas of this school and to be able to use its arguments, instruments and methodology. This approach demystified political decision-making processes, gave additional arguments for the explanation of "government failure" in both capitalism and communism, and sharpened the understanding of the irrationalities of engineering methods when applied to the regulation of economic and social processes.

As I said, the public choice school was of great importance for the criticism of the old command economy (and society). It was, however, no less important in our search for the rational and easiest way to transform it, to create a free society and a market economy. We did not have the slightest confidence in the capacity of the government and its representatives to centrally plan and command the economy, nor did we believe in their capacity to mastermind the transformation of such a society. We knew that fundamental systemic change is in reality a very delicate mixture of intentions on the side of the politicians, and the spontaneous behavior of millions of free "players" in the political and economic field. Therefore, we decided to privatize, deregulate and liberalize most of the activities which — in the past — were in the hands of the state.

Communism was — as is well-known — a society organized around maximizing political benefits and not economic efficiency, and we are still struggling with this legacy. Although we are — after eight years of radical systemic transformation — still on our way, we are, at the same time, surprised at how far and how fast we have already moved after so little change during 40 years of communism. Some of us are disappointed that life has not yet reached the smoothness and easiness that it has here in Tucson. As we see it now, we have to face a problem of enormous and necessarily unfulfilled expectations. Especially now, when basic transformation measures and dislocations have already been completed, we feel that the gap between expectations and reality — together with the relative carelessness of the people about the fragility of the free society — begins to negatively dominate the atmosphere in the country.

Contrary to post-1989 dreams and unjustified declarations (mostly from abroad), there is no such thing as a free reform. To move from one institutional setting to another has its non-zero costs and these costs must be paid. They must be paid at home (with the exception of East Germany) and they must be paid by all — whether they were victims or exponents of communism. The role of the rest of the world is in this respect close to zero and the marginal product of foreign aid has only exceptionally a positive sign.

We have to patiently explain at home the difference between romantic and realistic views of politics. There are, in our society, residual beliefs in the ability of the state to behave paternalistically and to guarantee happiness for everyone. This frame of mind has been, paradoxically, reinforced by the welfare state ideologies and methods in Western Europe (and America). A huge list of deficiencies and imperfections — as compared to the countries which did not undergo the same communist experiment — together with a special "catching-up flavor" make the problem more pressing than it would have been in a standard democratic society. Powerful and very vocal pressure groups, which you know so well from your own country, started in a short time to fill the gap between the government and the private sector, which is a very efficient way to block both rational behavior by the government and rational systemic evolution.

The public choice school helped us to understand the importance of the clear definition of the border between the private and the public, and warned us against the "society of interest groups" and against partialization and weakening of the state. We do want a limited but strong state, not an extensive (with fuzzy borders) and weak one. We, in Europe, have our disastrous experience with the consequences of the creeping metamorphosis of a free society into a corporativist (or syndicalist) one. With such a background, we look very carefully at the communitarian tendencies in your country and elsewhere. It is a mixed blessing and we feel its shortcomings. The constant threat is rooted in the fact that political processes in democracy allow organized interest groups to communicate their demands for government transfers and other forms of privileges and to capture important benefits by expanding government. And this is very dangerous.

There is no doubt that markets emerge wherever and whenever there exist opportunities for individuals to gain through exchange. (That is the reason why many explicit, but especially implicit, markets existed even in the communist society.) Markets appear whether we want them or not, but for market activity to serve as the basis of general economic prosperity and of general human feelings of justice, they must exist within a body of law. We know that the quality of the rules of the game is probably the most significant determinant of economic performance. But we should not make inappropriate promises.

It is not possible to passively import the rules of the game and, as Douglas North keeps stressing, "many countries accepted the U.S. Constitution but function quite differently." It is, nevertheless, relatively easy to construct formal legislation (of course, under the pressure of organized interest groups, it is not quite so easy). It is, however, much more difficult to lay the foundations of its enforcement. We need working and performing institutions (courts, regulatory bodies, police, etc.) and we need informal rules (cultural traits and traditions) but they cannot be "introduced" by decree during the only partially and imperfectly organized transformation process. My experience tells me that the interaction of formal rules with institutions which are supposed to enforce them and with dominant informal rules is another critical factor affecting transformation costs.

To summarize, there are many problems at this moment of transition from communism to a free society, and there is no chance of guaranteeing a smooth transition path in a politically and socially difficult, but highly democratic, pluralistic and open economy and society. We are not in a "brave new world" of perfect markets and perfect governments. Nevertheless, we know we have to complete the transition as quickly as possible and avoid paying an unnecessarily high price for it.

Political Life with an Academic Mentality

Stanford University and Hoover Institution, Stanford, California, November 13, 1997

I have in my hands at least three explicit invitations to speak at Stanford — one from Anne Krueger, one from Michael Boskin and one from Kurt Leube. In my interpretation, the first one is about the experiences of a politician with an academic background, the second is about economics and economic policy issues in a transforming country and the third about free society and its enemies. All three topics are very inspiring, but I decided that I have to obey the "ladies first" principle and start with some recollections of a politician who wanted to be an academic economist.

I came to politics at the age of 48 without thinking about it and without consciously preparing for it. Such an unexpected entry onto the political scene was possible only at the moment of a revolution (luckily a velvet one in our case) and in this respect it is unrepeatable and can not be imitated. Such rapid evolution of a political career — from the position of the minister of finance to the chairmanship of a newly established political party and finally to the position of the prime minister, all within less than three years — would be probably impossible in a standard political setting.

On the other hand, life in the communist system was highly politicized, the horizontal relationships of individuals and institutions at the micro level were suppressed (or blocked), everything was done in the vertical scheme, and therefore, everything was political. Paradoxically, we were excessively political because we were constantly talking about the irrationalities of the old system. Although such debates were rather theoretical and abstract, and we never envisaged entering politics in the future, on the "day after" it happened we suddenly became politicians. The preconditions for the success of our entry into politics included:

- the profound and conceptual understanding of the old communist system and its unconditional rejection and refusal (much stronger than within the Western academic community);
- no flirtations with any variants of slippery "Third Ways," with convergence theories, with social engineering dreams, with technocratic, constructivistic approaches to finding solutions to human problems;

- oversensitivity as regards various elements of creeping socialism in Western societies;
- a clear vision of where to go;
- no "pretense of knowledge" (in the Hayekian sense) and no ambitions to mastermind either the economy (or society), or the transition process from communism to a free society. To put it differently, we believed in the spontaneity of social processes, which is something we are permanently criticized for.

I would like to stress my strong conviction that there is a special advantage in studying economics, which gives a much different and, in my opinion, more productive *instrumentarium*, or intellectual tools, than other social sciences. I have in mind its methodology, its main conclusions, its dispute between market and plan or between monetarism and Keynesianism, the ideas of public finance and especially of the public choice school, the invaluable contributions of the economics of property rights and of transactions costs, the works of Friedman, Stigler, Becker, Buchanan, Tullock and many others.

I consider extremely important the ability of those who are genuine economists:

- to simplify complex problems and to concentrate on crucial issues;
- to deal efficiently with statistics;
- to strictly distinguish positive and normative thinking;
- to divide variables into exogenous and endogenous, to separate economic categories into constants and variables, to subconsciously and immediately differentiate between the short, medium and long run (in economist Alfred Marshall's approach), etc.;
- to apply economic thinking not only to explicit markets;
- to be aware of transaction costs, and in particular of the fact that there are major transaction costs in delegating authority to others, and that there are transaction costs whenever we move to a new institutional setting (there is, of course, no such thing as a free reform);
- the idea of the margin, i.e., that most decisions involve a little more or little less, etc.

Without having these basic but non-trivial principles "deeply rooted," it is impossible to be a good academic economist or a good politician.

To illustrate the close connection between economics and politics, I would like to share with you one unique problem we encountered during the transformation in the Czech Republic — the problem of huge and necessarily unfulfilled expectations connected with the end of communism. The gap between expectations and reality has undergone several dramatic switches between 1989 and now and I will try to make some generalizations about it.

In the first period, immediately after the unexpected collapse of communism in November 1989 (unexpected in its rapidity and deepness), the expectations-reality gap, let's call it the e-r gap, either did not exist at all or was in the opposite direction (r>e). The suddenly achieved freedom was valued so highly that no clouds on the horizon were seen or envisaged. Everyone assumed (and I have to admit that the politicians — for understandable reasons — did not warn sufficiently against it) that transformation had almost no costs. Everyone assumed that the release of the latent human energy after the elimination of all political, economic and bureaucratic barriers would bring gains that would be bigger than costs connected with the dismantling of the old system. Such assumptions were over-optimistic because transformation costs were — inevitably — non-zero.

In the second period, from 1989 to 1993, the transformation costs became apparent and somebody had to bear them. The rapid adjustment to a standard economic structure was composed of both contraction and expansion, but the contraction (I used to call it the *transformation shakeout*) was — especially at the beginning — much bigger than the simultaneous expansion of new activities. Between 1989 and 1993 industrial output fell by 33.6 percent, agricultural output by 23.5 percent and GDP by 21.4 percent. There was, at the same time, a very rapid growth of services, but their contribution did not make up for the decline in the primary and secondary sectors of the economy.

As a result, the e-r gap widened, but at that time we succeeded in explaining and defending our policies. There were, of course, attempts to argue that a more gradual approach would have been less costly but we were — and are — convinced that so-called gradualism would have produced new dangerous distortions. No less important was the fact that the markets both at home and abroad were not "gradualistically" waiting for such experiments and that something like a sophisticated gradualism could not have been realized in a complex, pluralistic, democratic, open society. There was, therefore, no other way out but to go ahead and introduce all deregulation, liberalization and privatization measures as fast as possible. I stress complex, pluralistic, democratic and open, because I am convinced that in such a world there is no room for social engineering and that there is no one who has the mandate, knowledge and capacity to do it. I fully agree with Milton Friedman that "the error of supposing that the behavior of social organisms can be shaped at will is widespread. It is the fundamental error of most so-called reformers. It explains why they so often feel that the fault lies in the man, not the *system*."

The third period, which in our case started in 1993, was characterized by relatively rapid GDP growth and by the apparent growth of real personal incomes (especially wages). In the period 1992 to 1996 the growth of real wages reached 32.3 percent. Because of low unemployment, we enjoyed a relative social peace. The e-r gap was lessened and, as a result, the ruling coalition succeeded twice in winning the parliamentary elections — which is an achievement unique in the post-communist world. However, the elections in 1996 were very narrow, mostly because when they took place, we were already at the beginning of the next period.

The fourth period started when basic transformation measures and dislocations had already been completed. Because of that, more or less standard problems of a free society and market economy, together with relative carelessness on the part of citizens about the fragility of a free society, began to dominate the societal atmosphere, but with the following, unpleasant qualifications:

- As an inevitable heritage from the communist era, there remains a huge list of unsatisfied demands. Our fellow citizens want to be "in Europe" already, now. Their collectivistic organizations — trade unions, professional chambers and similar entities — are involved in standard rent-seeking, and in doing so they push for collectivistic solutions to meet their demands;
- Our health care system, which is partly privatized, excessively based on output or performance incentives (which leads inevitably to the oversupply of health care) and on overall compulsory health insurance, is running out of money and needs a radical systemic change;
- Government bureaucracy is slower in understanding all the magic and all the fallacies of the market mechanism than its individual participants at the micro level. As a result, economic agents are able to use or misuse all the deficiencies of the still immature, shallow markets and the government is — necessarily — blamed for that;

- We have opened ourselves to the rest of the world more than the rest of the world to us. That creates difficult problems with our balance of trade and it complicates the life of some of our industries (rapidly growing imports of heavily subsidized agricultural and food products from Europe, increasing imports of extensively export-promoted products of the European manufacturing sector, the impact of foreign department store chains with their biased product structure, etc.);
- The government and the private sector are squeezed between powerful and very vocal pressure groups which — together with the left-wing political opposition — succeeded in converting the atmosphere in the country and in widening the e-r gap.

Looking into the future, *the fifth period* will be characterized either by the continuation of existing, more or less consistent transformation policies and the subsequent reversal of the e-r gap, or by a fall into the blind alley of populism and empty symbolism with all their well-known consequences.

I hope we will keep on moving ahead.

Transition from Communism: A Decade After

Lovett C. Peters Lecture at the Pioneer Institute for Public Policy Research, Boston, April 21, 1999

It is an honor to address this distinguished audience and an honor to be invited by the Pioneer Institute — even if the term "pioneer" was for me most of my life connected with one special meaning: with the communist youth organization with its red scarves and with marching in the First of May parade.

It does not seem very productive to describe events which happened 10 years ago at the moment of the end of communism or to repeat the famous debates about where to go and how to get there. We have to go further now. I would like, therefore, first to put the transition problem into a broader perspective of the general ideological framework of our times and then to discuss several selected aspects of the process of transition.

1. The Re-Emergence of New Third Ways

We are very rapidly approaching the end of the century and the beginning of a new one. I do not like strong and easy but sometimes deceptive words and concepts; however, they may be appropriate when talking about the 20th century. We can say — at least looking at the world from Central Europe — that the 20th century brought us two wars, two occupations of our own territories and two dangerous ideologies — fascism and communism. We were three times liberated — from the Austro-Hungarian autocratic monarchy in 1918, from German occupation in 1945 and from communism in 1989. Only three decades — the '20s, the '30s and the '90s — were episodes of freedom and liberty — which is approximately one-third of the whole century. Knowing the circumstances, it is very difficult to say whether it is a good result or a bad one. And especially as compared to whom or to what other era of our history?

I agree with Isaiah Berlin, who once said that "horrors in the 20th century were not caused by the ordinary negative human sentiments; they have been caused by ideas." This is — at least for me — a very important point. I am really more afraid of some ideas than of nasty people, of wicked or evil persons, of villains. And I am sensitive to the dangers of personalizing history — the current Yugoslav crisis notwithstanding. And even if communism is over, I am not the only one who sees, hears and feels other ideas that are dangerous. We should not, therefore, interpret the end of communism as a final and comfortable victory. We should be "on guard."

Contrary to the "end of history" or "end of ideology" schools, *the end of communism does not mean the end of the great ideological debate which dominated the 20th century*. It began one. Or it should have. The debate should have taken place much earlier and should have been deeper and subtler, but communism distracted us from it. Looking around in America, in Europe, in my own country, I do not have the feeling that someone like me (or the supporters of the Pioneer Institute) is on the winning side. I agree with one of the few French liberals (in the European sense), Pascal Salin, that "we are not the winners of the present time. So far the victory is that of social democracy." He is right. He sees Mr. Clinton, Mr. Blair, Mr. Jospin, Mr. Schroeder, Mr. Prodi (the new Mr. Europe), and I see Mr. Zeman and Mr. Havel in my own country. They all belong to the same club, at least implicitly.

The "Third Way" ideas are here again and I have to repeat my well-known phrase coined in January 1990: "The Third Way is the fastest way to the Third World." We should not fall into the same trap as in the past. But some of the traps are different — I have to mention especially environmentalism and communitarianism. Both of them represent a danger to freedom, liberty and democracy; both of them imply that someone's ideas are better than the ideas of the rest of us and that someone knows what is good for me and you.

All of this is relevant for mature developed countries, for emerging markets in developing countries and for transition economies as well.

2. The Problems of Transition

The decade of the '90s started with many high hopes connected with the fact that communism collapsed. I always add that communism was not defeated, it — sort of — melted down. This long-awaited event created enormous expectations and led to an expectation-reality gap, or e-r gap.[1] In spite of many undeniable achievements in most transition countries during the past decade, the e-r gap has *been growing*. This in turn has led to a serious loss of confidence, both in transformation results and in transformation strategies. Dramatic controversy about it continues and will be with us for some time to come.

I am sorry to say that the Western intellectual contribution to this debate has not been very helpful. There has been almost no serious academic research concerning transition from communism to a free society, and the quality of available texts is not much better than the former sovietologist literature which we — living in communism — did not find very helpful either. We learned a lot from ideas and concepts belonging to mainstream economics but were not enriched by a more or less descriptive sovietologist literature which was usually less sophisticated than our own (which was done in a much more complicated environment). It seems to me now that *almost everyone forgot the evils and irrationalities of communism* and is surprised that its dismantling is not fast enough and that it takes non-zero time to replace it with a full-fledged market economy.

The academic analysis is made up for by a nonacademic one. The debate about transition economies (and emerging markets) is dominated by a very powerful rent-seeking group of advisers and consultants, of investment bankers, of powerful auditors and especially of bureaucrats of international financial organizations who have a vested interest in prolonging transition as much as possible, and in not letting transition countries do it domestically (which means without them). My refusal to unconditionally surrender to their views and my statement "I am not ready to pay hard money for soft advice" (which Milton Friedman dubbed "Klaus' law") made me many enemies in this privileged group.

I have expressed my views about transition (and described my experience with it) in many speeches and articles and it is probably too early to add anything to my original "Ten Commandments of Transition."[2] I will, therefore, only make some short remarks:

- To paraphrase the well-known saying (ascribed to Milton Friedman), "there is no such thing as a free reform." *The change of the whole system is very costly.* The transformation costs consist of *the loss of output* (and income), *the fundamental redistribution of gains and losses in society*, *an increase of inequality in income and wealth, the loss of behavioral patterns*, etc. These costs have to be paid by citizens of the transforming countries themselves and the contribution of the rest of the world is marginal (if any and if not a negative one);
- The reforms usually started with emphasis on liberalization, deregulation and privatization. Such reforms can be implemented quite rapidly. The implementation of such reform measures is of crucial importance, but at the beginning they created weak and shallow markets and imperfect market infrastructure. The inefficient (or not fully efficient) markets and surrounding institutions increased transformation costs and added something unexpected to the unpleasant feelings of less successful participants in the transition process. We are, therefore, heavily criticized for weak markets and imperfect institutions, but there was no other way to proceed.

In addition, our distrust of the state and its potential constructive contribution was much stronger in our part of the world than in yours. In the past we suffered more from "government failure" than you and we believed that market failure is much smaller and less dangerous than the failure of government. Karl Brunner once said that the state should be "an umpire of a positive sum game and not an operator of a negative sum game" and we accepted this approach as a guideline in our reform strategy;

- Many reforms failed or had very high costs because they were not completed and because of the time-inconsistency problem connected with the fact that individual reform measures have different time dimensions. This is an unavoidable fact of life which should not be so superficially criticized as it is usually done with the highbrow approach of those who either do not care or have their own interests;
- We understood very soon the fallacy of the artificially introduced dilemma called "shock therapy vs. gradualism" which used to be so popular in the literature. I can confirm that the systemic change is *a sequence of many distinct choices over time on separate components of an overall reform plan* and not a single decision. It takes a whole historic period. It is not an exercise in applied economics. The systemic change is not done in a laboratory or in a vacuum, it is done inside a very complicated political process in an open, democratic and pluralistic society (there is no masterminding of it).

What are the main future dangers?

We should be aware of the fact that a country in the moment of transition does not make *marginal* changes (as a non-transition country), it makes *substantial* changes. This is a crucial difference. There has not been a long, gradual, spontaneous evolution of institutions, rules or networks of relations based on the enormous variety of human interests, hopes, dreams and ambitions as in your country. Because of that, we still live in a "pre-emptied" system which does not have the friendly, softening mechanisms of intermediation between invisible hands of the market and visible hands of the government. Such an intermediate structure cannot be imposed upon society from above, it has to evolve. In our society, the strong and noisy pressure groups often succeed in using legislation to gain powers and privileges at the expense of both individual citizens and the state, and to shift society from traditional liberal democracy to neocorporativism. It has an important connection to the currently fashionable idea of *communitarianism.*

Communitarianism is less dangerous in a mature, sufficiently diversified society but may very easily refeudalize an immature (and in this respect shallow) society.[3]

A second future problem is connected with the existing (and unavoidable) fragility and vulnerability of transition economies — especially when they are confronted with the growing and merciless requirements of a globalized environment. The transition countries have particular propensities, especially to higher inflation and to current account deficits which are not compatible with fixed (and stable) exchange rates.[4] Transition economies have, at the same time, investment-savings imbalances and need foreign capital to ensure some sort of macroeconomic equilibrium. However, foreign capital wants fixed exchange rates and easy outflow possibilities. All of that does not simultaneously exist and will probably never exist.

My experience tells me that the reconciliation of all those variables cannot be masterminded *ex ante*. It must be enforced upon the economy *ex post*, as a result of economic, financial and currency instability (or crisis). It brings about, however, a politically and socially very complicated situation and, as a result, the political support for the continuation of transformation is undermined. This is what we have seen in recent years in many countries, and, paradoxically, more often in more successful transition economies.

The problems of transition can be discussed with many details and from many perspectives. Transition is a very complicated mixture of political, social, economic and cultural aspects and a mixture of intended and unintended moves and events. I wanted to warn against their underestimation, against various misinterpretations, against false labels such as "the absence of the rule of law," "crony capitalism," "mafia capitalism," etc. I wanted to present it as a painful process connected with dreams, hopes, ambitions, prejudices, fears and, of course, human errors. I agree with the Hayekian statement that the world is run by human action, not by human design. We should not forget it.

Ten Years After: First Lessons Drawn

Prague Castle, Czech Republic, November 18, 1999

With the benefit of hindsight, with the advantage of 10 years' experience, with all the victories and losses, pluses and minuses, successes and disappointments, we can dare to make first generalizations — as regards both political and economic aspects of the transition from communism to a free society and market economy. Let me use this opportunity to address this topic.

A. The Political Side

We can make a strong point that an open, pluralistic and democratic society has been created.

All transformation measures have been done by democratically formed political structures, at least in the Central and East European region, where political pluralism, parliamentary democracy, competition of political parties, unconstrained freedom of the media, etc., fully dominate (it is probably not the case when we move more to the East or South);

It suggests that transition was not masterminded from above, that it was not dictated by one autocratic politician or another, that it was the product of a very specific and complicated mixture of intentions and spontaneity, of design and of action, of planned and unplanned events;

It is easy to criticize the outcome of such an evolutionary and uncontrolled process from the outside (as uninvolved observers), from the standpoint of abstract theories or vested interests, from absolutistic ideological principles. But the transition was not an exercise in applied economics, it was "real life" — with all its contradictions and ambivalences.

The task of politicians was to get support for transition; some of us succeeded, some of us did not. Our success or failure, however, dramatically influenced the level of transformation costs (this is what we call the costs of undergoing transition);

What did the politicians have to do?

The politicians had to defend or rehabilitate the role of political parties (the word "party" was totally discredited in the communist era) and to block acceptance of "Third Way" thinking based on loose, fuzzy organizations like civic movements, national fronts for or against something or somebody;

My experience tells me that there is a strong correlation between the presence of a standard political structure (with well-defined political parties) and the success of transition (and I believe history will prove that I was right);

The politicians had to fight the romantic or pseudo-romantic point of view which holds that:

- It is possible (when changing society) to look for new, unknown, untried solutions, and to use the collapse of communism as an opportunity for creating another utopia; and that
- It is possible to get something for nothing, that there is such a thing as a free reform, and there are no transformation costs.

I believe that the last 10 years demonstrated that both ideas were and are wrong, but we have to admit that it has not been fully accepted, either in the post-communist world or in the rest of the world. Because of that the expectations–reality gap (e-r gap) has been steadily growing, not narrowing. There is no doubt that much has been accomplished in this past decade. We have witnessed an enormous change in the basic substance of life in most of the transition countries, but *the expectations have been growing even faster.* The road from communism to free society and market economy is rocky, nevertheless some people do not want to take into consideration that there is no magic carpet which can avoid the necessity of our travelling it. To my great regret, such a fairy tale is still here. I have to say that this fairy tale is supported by activities of international consultants and advisers, of investment bankers, of bureaucrats of international organizations who pretend that the only missing factor is listening to their advice. They represent, however, a very well functioning rent-seeking group. Additional problems come from inside. For some people, feeling bad feels so good that they invest a lot in criticism, skepticism and the creation of a bad mood. To fight such attitudes represents a challenge which the politicians very often do not win. At least in my country.

A serious discussion of the political aspects of transition would require us to deal with several other important, nontrivial issues. I will just name a few of them:

a) Transition is a sequence of policy decisions, not a once-for-all policy change (the wrong debate is about gradualism versus shock-therapy);

b) Transition is based on human choices (influenced by ideas, prejudices, dreams and interests), not on scientific knowledge (the Hayekian point about human action versus human design);

c) Transition brings democracy, but more democracy typically enhances the power of interest groups in general, and blocks further reforms in particular;

d) During the transition from communism, the first problem was to concentrate on solving the dichotomy between oppression and freedom, whereas the no-less-important dichotomy between anarchy and order was usually neglected or at least underestimated, especially in the early period;

e) The critical factor affecting transformation costs is the interaction of formal versus informal rules on the one hand and the gap between rules and their implementation on the other.

B. The Economic Side

The challenges for every transition economy in the economic field at the very beginning were manifold:

- to minimize the inevitable economic decline which followed the fundamental change of economic conditions (they were partly the result of the transformation strategy itself and partly the unintended consequence of the altered international environment);
- to eliminate the inherited excess demand (or forced savings) at the moment of price liberalization without initiating galloping inflation or even hyperinflation;
- to liberalize prices and foreign trade without creating difficult social conditions and economic imbalances;
- to deregulate markets even if there continued to be a very imperfect market structure;
- to privatize state ownership rapidly, efficiently, with domestic participation and in a socially tolerable way;
- to change institutions, rules and legislation as fast as possible but in a democratic (and constitutional) way.

1. *Managing the first stage of transition, when the costs greatly exceeded the benefits (at least in an economic sense)*

Transition economies succeeded in the above-mentioned tasks with mixed results. I have no ambition to analyze other countries, as such analyses are usually very superficial. Instead, I will concentrate on the Czech economy.

The Czech Republic´s transformation shakeoff led to a visible output loss: it amounted to 1/3 of industrial output, 1/4 of agricultural output and 1/5 of GDP. The figures are relatively high, but they are lower than the figures in most of the transition countries and, what is even more important, there was no way to avoid it.

Due to a lesser inflationary imbalance we "enjoyed" during the communist era and due to very cautious and restrictive macroeconomic policy after its end but prior to price liberalization, the highest rate of inflation was "only" 57 percent (in the year of price liberalization) and it rapidly declined to a 10 percent annual rate in the following years.

As a result of restrictive monetary and fiscal policy and sharp devaluation of the crown before foreign trade liberalization, there was not a dangerous trade imbalance and thus it was not necessary to stop its development by introducing administrative measures.

It is difficult to say only a few words about privatization without caricaturing it. It needs a special lecture which I am not able to deliver now. I would at least like to differentiate transformation privatization and classical privatization and to mention the Czech Republic's voucher privatization program.

To summarize the first stage of transition, we can say that we succeeded in minimizing the gap between costs and benefits, in avoiding the price-wage-price or price-exchange rate-price spirals that we had been so much afraid of, in dismantling old institutions and in minimizing social difficulties.

2. Managing the second stage, when the benefits started to exceed the costs

The main feature of the second stage was the resumption of economic growth. In the Czech Republic:

- It led to a real wage increase of one-third;
- It led to a rapid growth of the tertiary (services) sector, to a visible improvement in environment and infrastructure;
- It was characterized by an extremely high investment ratio, an investment-saving imbalance, a growing trade deficit, a massive inflow of foreign capital and, gradually, a deteriorating balance of payments.

Relatively rapid growth, a balanced budget, low inflation and an uninterrupted inflow of foreign capital made us relatively comfortable, and we did not see the first "warning" signals of the growing imbalance, which — in a small, open economy — leads not to domestic inflation but to balance of payments (current account) difficulties.

3. Managing the growing imbalance: hard landing because of insensitive macroeconomic policies

The task of the government, and especially of the monetary authorities, was to slow down the growth of domestic aggregate demand and to ensure "a soft landing." We did not succeed. The central bank made a fundamental mistake, and its "overkill" destabilized the economy.

The standard anatomy of a currency crisis developed:

- collapses within the banking sector;
- growing uncertainty among foreign investors (and especially speculators);
- the start of a decline in economic growth (with a standard lag after the change of monetary policy);
- falling budget revenues, prompting government attempts to balance the budget by cutting expenditures (which contributed to the decline of demand);
- an attack on the crown (with the absence of a pre-attack abandonment of the fixed-exchange rate);
- 10 percent devaluation and the huge loss of currency reserves;
- political instability;
- extreme vulnerability of the banking and financial sector, leading to many bank failures;
- continuation (and even reinforcement) of the restrictive monetary policy in the form of high real interest rates and stricter reserve requirements (and other similar regulatory measures);
- credit crunch.

4. *Another Upturn?*

We are hopefully approaching the turning point based upon the growth of consumption and exports. However, the resumption of investment growth has not yet arrived. It depends on the change of climate in the banking sector. The change itself depends on the acceptance by the central bank, foreign investors and international financial institutions that our banking problems reflect the current macro situation rather than the systemic issues. We are, however, far from reaching such a consensus.

Conclusion

Transition is not an easy task. It is a unique historic event, in many respects unparalleled in recent history. We should not pretend *now* that it would have been possible to do things differently.

Economic and Political Trends in the Czech Republic

National Center for Policy Analysis conference, Balleroy, France, April 16, 2002

It is now exactly 12 years after the collapse of communism in the Czech Republic and in the other countries of Central and Eastern Europe. We constantly ask ourselves, of course, whether we used this period fully, in an optimal way, or whether much more could have been achieved. My answer is that *we have already succeeded in creating something like a basic stage of the system of parliamentary democracy and market economy and in liquidating all the structures and mechanisms of the former communist society. This is quite an achievement.*

We have also learned some important lessons that were not completely evident or widely accepted 12 years ago. We have learned, for example, that it is difficult for the people of the country undergoing transition *to differentiate between systemic change and a catching up* to *the current stage of development in countries* which did not go through the communist undertaking or experiment. Because of that, the original, undoubtedly unique and unrepeatable euphoria did not last long and we sometimes face impatience and disillusion now. But it is not nostalgia for the old regime as it is sometimes claimed, especially abroad.

We have also learned that some changes were easier than we expected but that some other changes were much more difficult, if not impossible to realize. We can say that *we did not succeed in creating a free society as the NCPA would define it.* I will try to explain what I mean by that.

Eleven years ago, I accepted as a title of my speech in Sydney, Australia, the rather provocative words "Dismantling Socialism: A Preliminary Report."[5] I did not protest against the word "socialism," either because I was not careful enough or because, at that time, I really believed in the possibility of the world-wide dismantling of socialism. *Instead of it, we have got something else.* We have got a World Wide Web, world-wide terrorism, the European Union and the euro, new, more sophisticated, more hidden and more intensive methods of government intervention and regulation, the ever-increasing size and scope of the welfare state, multiculturalism and political correctness. I know that it is not necessary to explain or emphasize this here, but it is not understood in many other places.

It would probably have been appropriate to speak about the *dismantling of communism.* In this respect, my speech today could be called "a final report," because *communism is over* — politically as well as economically.

Our experience tells us that it was relatively easy to change the political system and the whole political structure. Communism collapsed, and it was not necessary to violently stop or prohibit anything. It was sufficient to liberalize the entry into the political market. As a result, new political parties were created almost instantaneously and a political plurality was established without constructing (or designing) it. It was a spontaneous process, it was nobody's design.

It was much more difficult to change the economic system. As is well known, the starting point of the transition was *liberalization and the deregulation of markets.*

We began with *price liberalization* (after 40 years of frozen and administered prices), with *foreign trade liberalization* (replacing the state monopoly on foreign trade and opening up the semiautarkic, protected economy) and with the *liberalization of entry into the market* for all types of enterprises (private as well as foreign).

To realize changes of that type was socially difficult, politically brave, but technically relatively easy. Most of the changes required nothing more than being announced.

The second stage of transition asked for more activity on the part of the government. It was necessary to establish new institutions and organizations, and to transform the old ones.

The main issue in this respect was privatization. It was impossible to wait for the slow emergence of hundreds or thousands of private enterprises and for the slow disappearance of state-owned firms, which 12 years ago in the former Czechoslovakia represented almost 100 percent of the whole economy.

It was necessary to privatize the state-owned firms on a massive scale, on a wholesale basis, which is something Western countries have never experienced. Nevertheless, your own experience with limited privatization tells you that privatization is difficult — both politically and technically. Whatever the government does and however it does it, the politicians are accused either of favoritism and selection of inappropriate new owners, or of not getting the best price.

Some unnecessary delays in privatization in my country were caused more by such fears and by the political infighting than by the ideologically motivated unwillingness to privatize. In any case, *privatization has been done and we have only several residual cases left to solve.*

Many people at home and abroad — the participants in the transformation process as well as the uninvolved observers — live even now in a very strange mental state, if not schizophrenia. They consider communism to be an absolute evil but, at the same time, they more or less assume that getting rid of it should be free, without costs, without tension, without ups and downs, without non-negligible lapses of time.

I have to disagree with this naive belief that taking away the old barriers, obstacles and constraints brings about immediate benefits — positive economic growth and increases in the standard of living, even in the short run. To put it graphically:

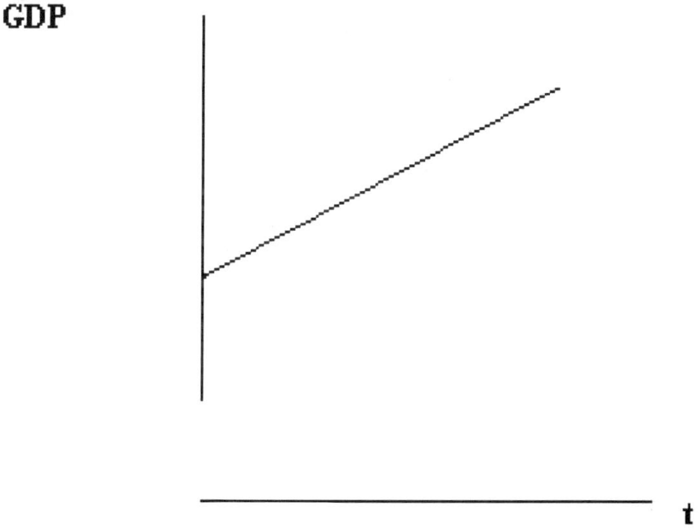

It did not materialize. It was complicated by the additional problem that many things have changed for the better but some of them were not visible in statistical indicators. (There is no way to incorporate freedom and the lack of shortages or queuing into GDP statistics.)

The Czech people slowly and reluctantly accepted the inevitability of what I call the *transformation shakeoff* — the huge loss of output, income, employment, price stability, prevailing distribution of income and property, existing degree

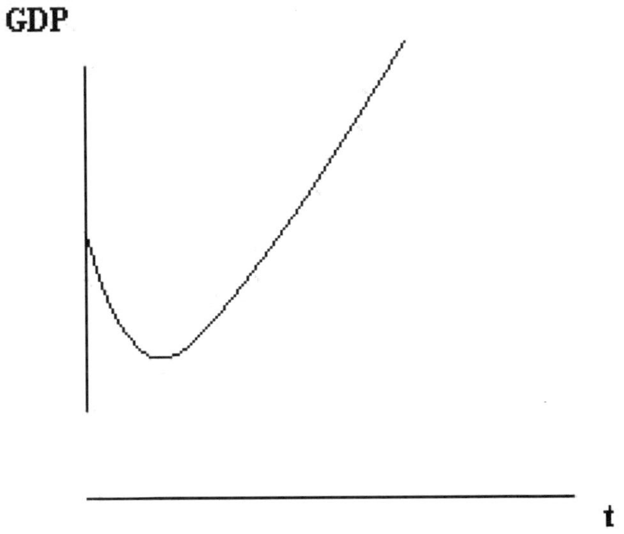

of social security, etc. But after that, they again made a mistake and expected more or less uninterrupted economic growth.

They were, of course, confronted with further problems.

In the mid-1990s, in the middle of worldwide currency crises (from Mexico and Southeast Asia to Russia) and with a growing external imbalance at home, the Czech National Bank unexpectedly (and without any consultation with the government) introduced very restrictive monetary measures which destabilized the economy, undermined the banking sector, made both domestic economic agents and foreign investors nervous, and produced a relatively small currency crisis. This was followed by an unpleasant economic recession which lasted for the next two or three years.

The Czech people did not expect it. They were (and are even now) very naively convinced that the market economy (as compared to central planning and state ownership) means — almost automatically — a success. They were not prepared psychologically for a business failure — either at the micro or macro level. They felt they had been cheated or betrayed by politicians who had sold them the idea of capitalism, free markets, liberalization, deregulation and privatization without sufficient warnings. (I don't think, however, that the selling of a new ideology could have been done differently.)

You know very well that, even in a mature, stable, developed market economy, success is not the only outcome. But it is even less true in a transition economy — with its dramatically changing economic environment, in competition with much stronger partners from the rest of the world, without sufficient experience.

The one who was blamed for business failures was the government, not the individuals owning and managing the firms. It became fashionable to argue that the failures were caused by unsuccessful privatization and an insufficient legislative and institutional framework.

Many advisers came to give us their recommendations. We were confronted with enormous naivete with regard to the formation of legislation, its enforcement, the relationship between formal legislation and informal rules, etc. We were criticized for our inability to create perfect legislation. It was forgotten that:

- there is no such thing as perfect legislation;
- the formation of legislation is and must be slow;
- legislation is the outcome of the process of evolution, not of anyone's dictate;
- legislation is not the outcome of abstract rationalism, but of a complicated political process;
- legislation is influenced not only by political or ideological arguments but also by vested interests, lobbying and rent-seeking.

Our critics probably assumed that we were still a totalitarian state, where the appropriate legislation could have been simply introduced. It was and is not true.

With all our problems, we already live in a totally different world. We live in the world of incremental changes, of standard political processes, of many imperfections but of standard democratic mechanisms to deal with those imperfections. *Perfect society is far away, communism is even farther.*

As I mentioned before, *we do not see, however, the end of socialism* — either in my country or elsewhere. *We may even be closer to it now than 10 years ago.* Because of their structural similarities, the fall of communism and the overall attack on its irrationalities temporarily weakened socialism. Unfortunately, the last decade did not bring us the end of it. The decade of the '90s can be described as a victory of social democratism, of various varieties of the Third Way, of communitarianism, of environmentalism, of the dictate of political correctness, of human rightism, of Europeanism, of corporativism, of NGOism. To put it in a generalized way, we see a victory of new collectivisms.

Ten years ago, the dominant slogan was: "deregulate, liberalize, privatize." Now the slogan is different: "regulate, adjust to all kinds of standards of the most developed and richest countries (regardless of your stage of development), listen to the partial interests of the NGOs (non-governmental organizations) and follow them, get rid of your sovereignty and put it into the hands of international institutions and organizations."

This brings me to Europe. Our transition goes parallel with a rapidly changing European landscape. We started our changes in the era of the EC, have continued them in the era of the EU and will finalize them in the era of the EMU (or EFU or EPU). As we see it, with all our oversensitivity inherited from the past, Europe is undergoing a radical change while the uninvolved or uninterested majority of Europeans do not care or do not pay sufficient attention to it. Intergovernmental cooperation by independent countries aiming at removing barriers to the movement of people, goods, money and ideas has been — slowly but surely — converted into a supranational European state aiming at the centralization of power in Brussels and at the elimination of European nation states. With the benign neglect of the majority of Europeans, a minority of pro-European activists and the EU bureaucracy can have a decisive voice.

No one in this room — I suppose — is against the opening up of societies and the elimination of all kinds of barriers and obstacles to the free, unconstrained exchange of ideas, people, goods and services, and money all over the world. Some of us know from our own personal experience what it means to live in closed, inward-looking, almost autarkic societies where any form of contact with the outside world was prohibited (or at least made very difficult). We know what it means to live in the world of barriers, obstacles, borders, prohibitions and — eventually — of permissions to be allowed to do something or to go somewhere. As a result of that experience, we have been dreaming for years and decades about being part of European open society.

My empirical observation is that the current European unification process is not predominantly about opening up. It is about introducing massive regulation and protection, about imposing uniform rules, laws and policies, about weakening standard democratic processes (which have evolved over centuries), about an increasing bureaucratization of life, etc.

I am very sensitive to both sides of this process. Twelve years ago, we wanted to go "back to Europe," to the freedom which we did not enjoy in the communist era. But this is not the same as the rush into the European Union which is currently the most visible and the most powerful embodiment of ambitions to create something else — supposedly better — than a free society.

The accelerated unification of Europe is in my opinion an unnecessary and insufficiently prepared process, which will bring more problems than solutions. It has become, however, a quasi-religious belief to see it as a panacea. Opposing European unification is dismissed as something nationalistic, undemocratic and reactionary, and anyone who dares to do so is put together with such names as Lukasenko or Milosevic.

I see dangers in creating such a Brave New World. To be proud of one's own nation (and flag) is not a symptom of nationalism or of "incorrect political behavior." It is a rational political and human stance.

We have always been an integral part of Europe and we want to be nothing more and nothing less than a self-governing nation in the European Union. I have to be explicit in saying that in spite of seeing it so sharply and with all our reservations, *we want to participate in the European integration process. There is no other choice left.* It is the only way to get international recognition and legitimization.

To sum up: looking at my country in April 2002, I can say that pluralistic parliamentary democracy and market economy are already there. The standard human problems remain.

Footnotes to Chapter I

[1] Václav Klaus, 1997 Annual Hayek Memorial Lecture, "The Transformation of the Czech Society: Retrospect and Prospect," Institute of Economic Affairs, London, June 17, 1997.

[2] Luncheon address delivered to the plenary meeting of the Group of Thirty, Vienna, April 1993; also published in *Renaissance: The Rebirth of Liberty in the Heart of Europe* (Washington, D.C.: Cato Institute, 1997).

[3] See the Alpbach Forum 1998 Seminar speech devoted to "Society and the Crisis of Liberalism," August 22, 1998; published in *Policy*, Vol. 14, No. 4, 1998, Center for Independent Studies, Sydney, Australia.

[4] See "Emerging Markets and Their Current Problems: The Czech Perspective," speech delivered at the Delhi School of Economics, New Delhi, March 11, 1999.

[5] See "Dismantling the State: A Preliminary Report," John Bonython Lecture, Center for Independent Studies, July 25, 1991, Sydney, Australia.

Chapter II:

THE ECONOMICS OF TRANSITION

Václav Klaus, Telč, Czech Republic, May 11, 2004.

Economic Transformation of the Czech Republic: The Challenges that Remain

Speech at the Institute of International Finance, Washington, D.C., September 29, 1996

In the last couple of years I have made several attempts to discuss — in a more theoretical way — the transformation of a former communist country into a free society and a market economy. My texts were widely published and discussed, both at home and abroad. Moreover, I was lucky to have an opportunity to put some of the ideas of liberal (I use the term in its original European sense) economists and other social scientists into practice.

We have in our country completed one difficult stage of the transformation process after almost seven years of radical restructuring of the whole political, social and economic system. The relevant questions are: How do we continue? Is the transformation over? Is there in our case a special role for the government as compared to its role in Western countries? What are the new challenges? What remains to be done?

There is no doubt that our society in all its dimensions is very different compared to what it was in the communist era. Some changes are visible at first sight, some not. There probably have been more changes in the "software" than in the "hardware" of the whole socioeconomic system, which may confuse some observers, but I am sure that the overall political, economic and social restructuring went better than had been expected (and I do not talk about the Czech Republic only).

In 1993 (and with some modifications, in 1995 again), I formulated my 10 commandments of systemic reform and I am quite happy that it is not necessary to rewrite them yet. They included the following postulates:

- the fundamental transformation of the whole society in a historically short period is a feasible task (which is a nontrivial conclusion because six or seven years ago when we started, many doubted such a possibility);
- there is no way to mastermind the whole transformation process and to accomplish the optimal sequencing of individual transformation measures;
- there is in reality no choice between the so-called shock therapy and gradualism. Both terms are very simplified concepts suitable for a journalist's discussion, but they should not be used in a serious argument;

- the crowding out of nonviable economic activities (and the consequent economic decline) represents an inevitable part of the transformation process;
- an important role is played by very early price liberalization, which must be straightforward and wide-ranging. The same is true of foreign trade liberalization;
- there is no economic law saying that the faster the economic restructuring (and privatization), the higher the rate of unemployment (just the opposite is true);
- two economic variables — wages and the exchange rate — are of crucial importance. At the very beginning of the transformation process these must be pushed down by restrictive macroeconomic policies to create the so-called "transformation cushions;"
- the post-transformation recovery and long-awaited catching-up process cannot be artificially accelerated or shifted in time;
- the rapid transformation privatization, which is something conceptually different from classical privatization, must be done at a very early stage of the whole process;
- the radical transformation (in a unique and nonrepeatable political atmosphere) should be used not only to dismantle old institutions of a command economy but to de-establish the institutions of a paternalistic, overregulated welfare state as well.

This is in a very condensed form both *a normative blueprint* and *a positive description* of the transformation process in the Czech Republic. We are now in a situation which can be described in the following way:

- the economy has been mostly privatized; the share of state ownership is relatively small and declining; the mass privatization is over; we have entered the era of serious ownership restructuring, which will lead to a gradual improvement in corporate governance and the efficiency of individual companies;
- the government is trying to avoid being involved in any form of micro-intervention — but the pressures of partial interests, of lobbying of all kinds, of corporativism and syndicalism, of patterns of paternalism imported from abroad are getting stronger because, after their initial weakness, these pressure groups have become consolidated and their strength has grown;
- the economy has started to grow, all macroeconomic figures (expressed in rates of growth) have positive signs, and economic growth around 5 percent per annum seems to be a feasible midterm prospect;

- the main bottleneck on the supply side is represented by the low unemployment rate (around 3 percent) and the resulting shortage of labor and a net inflow of foreign workers which restrains the rate of economic growth in the short run;
- relatively strong growth, low unemployment, rapid growth of wages, residual deregulation of prices, rapid adjustments of domestic prices to world prices, frequent changes in the structure of the economy with corresponding movements of relative prices, etc., bring about a continuation of inflation at around 8 to 10 percent per annum and further disinflation becomes very difficult;
- more than 60 months of a fixed nominal exchange rate from the end of 1990 to February 1996, together with a large inflow of foreign capital and a positive balance of payments, constrained the monetary policy of the central bank and made it more or less passive (which may be a good method to discipline ambitious monetary authorities). The introduction of a relatively wide margin for fluctuations in the exchange rate in the spring of 1996 changed the situation sharply. It led to a slowdown of money supply growth in the summer and autumn of 1996, which may be a positive contribution to the overall macroeconomic situation;
- strong demand for money, attempts to slow down the supply of money, fragility of the banking sector plus the financial weakness of many new, privatized or still state-owned firms keep both real interest rates and margins between interest rates on credit and deposits relatively high, which becomes another inflationary factor (of the cost push variety);
- fiscal policy is based on the undisputed goal of a balanced budget and plays in our context a highly stabilizing role; the budget's share of GDP has been continuously going down;
- rapid economic growth, very liberal import procedures, comparative advantages to foreign firms entering the Czech market (because of their economic strength they are able to offer better starting conditions), subsidized products from the EU (with the backing of various methods of export promotion).
- all of this pushes domestic demand for imports above the level of exports, which has led to a significant deficit in the balance of trade (which is only partially offset by a positive balance of services). Exports are, moreover, very vulnerable to world (and mostly European) economic conditions and to the different kinds of import restrictions existing everywhere, and to

> insufficient domestic export promotion. The trade deficit is, therefore, considered to be the most important single economic problem of the current period.

Until now I have been looking at the economy from the purely domestic economic side. Now, I wish to say a few words about the noneconomic issues and about the role of the external side of things.

Until very recently the relative speed and smoothness of the Czech transformation process (social and political stability, low inflation and unemployment, more or less balanced and "just" sharing of the transformation costs by the whole society, the ingenious voucher privatization method, etc.) guaranteed basic support for the sometimes popular, sometimes painful transformation measures.

Czech society accepted (and "survived") the negative "collapse effect" of the dismantling of old institutions and activities, and absorbed — with satisfaction — the positive "liberalization effects" connected with the opening of domestic and foreign markets (not only in an economic sense). Czech society now sees growing disparities in income and property (not everyone is on the winning side) and waits for a massive "wealth effect" of a normally functioning capitalist society and economy. In addition, inflation is more stubborn than everyone expected, voucher privatization is over, and more and more groups in society have successfully avoided paying their share of transformation costs. Those who cannot escape paying the costs blame the government for not defending them sufficiently, regardless of the existence of apparent overall income growth. As a result, the basic (more or less unstructured and unconditional) support has partially vanished — as is reflected in the results of the recent Czech parliamentary elections. The space for brave government measures is, therefore, narrower than before.

Finally, a few words on the role of the rest of the world in this complicated process:

Basic political support, macroeconomic standby arrangements and direct help were extremely important, especially at the beginning. They are of secondary importance now. I do not deny the positive role of learning from abroad, but I have to insist that learning by doing (which means direct involvement in business with foreigners) has been much more important than professional consulting and advisory activity, because the first is a two-way process, and the second a one-way, nonbinding, nonfocused, nonmarket one.

The non-negligible external obstacle to our development comes from various forms of protectionism we face in various markets, including the markets of EU countries, CEFTA countries and other developed or developing nations. In spite of all of the promising rhetoric, the results are not that good. The current fashionable idea of fair trade instead of free trade may become very dangerous.

It is our duty, the duty to all of us, to promote free trade as much as possible — and I add, on both sides of the foreign trade equation. Not only on the import side (which is a usual argument), but also on the export side (all forms of state subsidies and export promotion).

Foreign investors are extremely important, but they should not expect advantages vis-à-vis domestic firms. To give these advantages is not the way to build a healthy economy.

We are willing to be a full member of the European Union (not an external observer). This is serious and, at home, undisputed. Our membership in the European Union remains, therefore, our most important external challenge.

The Process of Transition in Central and Eastern Europe: Its Revolutionary and Evolutionary Parts

Keynote speech at the Third Annual Eastern Europe/Russia ING Conference, Vail, Colorado, February 1998

Discussing Central and Eastern Europe in the spring of 1998, it seems appropriate to mention both the non-negligible and undeniably positive results which have been achieved in the transition economies of Central and Eastern Europe during the last eight years, and at the same time the no less undeniable problems connected with such a unique historical maneuver — the move from communism to a free society. There are many important, substantial similarities among the transforming countries, but we know as well that it is sometimes difficult to discover them because of the obvious differences we see at first sight. I will, nevertheless, try to generalize and outline broader tendencies (or lessons), even if I have to build on the Czech experience more than on the experience of other countries.

At the very beginning, eight years ago, in practically all the countries in question, very optimistic forecasts and expectations prevailed. They helped to initiate radical domestic reforms and to attract investors from abroad. Even if the structure of the transformation process was not identical in all the countries, crucial reforms have been realized, and they were, I hope, basically understood. Transformation activity was directed at the following tasks:

- *to liberalize* (trade, investment and prices);
- *to deregulate* (markets);
- *to privatize* (state property),

as fast and as comprehensively as possible, on the condition that one is able to pursue sufficiently restrictive macroeconomic policies. Some of us knew that to loosen fiscal and monetary controls, when economic imbalances (inherited from the communist past) dominated the macroeconomy, would have been destabilizing and would have led us into what I used to call the reform trap.

Everyone was aware of the fact that there had to be a *parallel evolution of the appropriate institutional infrastructure* — which when functioning minimizes the inevitable transaction costs and makes the market economy efficient and "just." However, this evolution was not achievable as fast as the liberalization and deregulation processes for many understandable reasons.

With the benefit of hindsight, we now know that:

- the institution-building process takes years, if not decades, which is a otally different time dimension than in the case of price or foreign trade liberalization;
- the government was so discredited after our communist experience that nobody believed it was capable of positive constructive activity (and nobody knew how to do so);
- some of us believed in the Hayekian process of spontaneous evolution of "extended orders" (as opposed to "made orders") and understood that it was impossible to stop this evolution, to stop the spontaneous behavior of millions of market "players" and to wait for the emergence of a perfect market infrastructure. Perhaps it can be done in a laboratory, but not in the real world.

As is well known, *ideas have consequences.* In this respect it is relevant that the whole transformation process started at a moment when the economic profession believed in several then-fashionable ideas:

- a government failure is much bigger than a market failure (therefore, deregulate — or, in our case, do not start to excessively regulate);
- fixed exchange rates represent a reliable nominal anchor for a transition economy;
- privatization has no costs and can be done by means of standard procedures;
- politicians should be able to guarantee the rational sequencing of individual reform measures, etc.

It seems to me that some of these ideas survived the decade, but some of them are not so fashionable now as they were before.

In the first stage, the reform steps "worked." After a short and inevitable economic decline which lasted two or three years and represented the healthy shakeout of nonviable economic activities associated with the old economic system, the economy began to recover. The rate of GDP growth reached the 4 to 6 percent range in the years that followed (three consecutive years in our case), the investment ratio became extremely high, domestic spending visibly grew, imports skyrocketed, and foreign capital inflows were enormous (as a share of GDP).

I have to admit that I believed in the possibility of a longer continuation of such a relatively smooth development — not in a fully linear way, but with only modest fluctuations. The experience of the last two years (let's call them the second stage) tells us, however, that we have underestimated the enormous vulnerability of such an economy (even if I think that it was probably more our incapacity to change the whole situation than our underestimation of this vulnerability). The economy was characterized by:

- dangerously growing expectations of all economic agents (consumers as well as investors) and our inability to slow them down without heavy political costs;
- overinvestment (from the macroeconomic point of view), both in directly productive and nondirectly productive activities, which led to an investment-saving disequilibrium;
- a growing trade imbalance, which was gradually accompanied by balance of payments' current account deficits;
- slow improvements in the institutional framework, by weak regulation of monopolistic or otherwise imperfect markets and by unsystematic law enforcement;
- disturbances connected with aggressive and merciless global capital markets, especially when they are confronted with weak domestic banking and financial intermediation.

As a result of all this, the second stage led to an economic slowdown (or stagnation) and to a political crisis, which meant the interruption of the previous, relatively smooth economic development.

The whole problem was created by underlying structural factors, but the trigger was the fact that markets became nervous about both the trade deficit and the strong currency (based on the nominal fixed exchange rate and on domestic inflation that was higher than the rates in OECD countries). As a result, capital inflows stopped, interest rates rose, the economy slowed down, tax revenues declined, fiscal balance deteriorated, budget expenditures had to be dramatically cut, the economy slowed down even more, capital was pulled out of the country, the currency depreciated, some firms and banks got into trouble, the economy went into very sluggish growth, etc. The anatomy of this crisis was rather simple (and well-known).

This story could be presented in a more extensive version, but the basic lesson is clear and straightforward. It was not identical in all the countries, but the most "clean" case was perhaps — to my great regret — the Czech Republic because of:

- its higher degree of openness and deregulation;
- more extensive financial transactions originally connected with voucher privatization;
- the insufficiency of capital market regulation;
- its extremely high investment ratio (33 percent in 1996);
- 75 months of a stable nominal exchange rate;
- a very restrictive step in monetary policy introduced in the middle of 1996;
- greater and faster growing expectations than elsewhere.

There is no doubt that we are slowly moving to the third stage. It will be characterized by consolidation and macroadjustment, residual privatization and institutional maturing. It is the period when the "first generation" reforms are over (with only some remaining "residuals") and when the "second generation" reforms will be realized. I am moderately optimistic in this respect, with two necessary qualifications:

First, I do not believe that the second stage could have been eliminated. I do not believe in the possibility of a smooth and stable transition path in the politically and socially difficult, but highly democratic, pluralistic and open societies (and economies) of Central and Eastern Europe. We are not in a "brave new world" of perfect markets and perfect governments. The current adjustment (or realignment) was necessary, but I am not sure that the changes could have been made "voluntarily," that they could have been intentionally "introduced." The adjustment had to be involuntary and therefore enforced.

Second, I agree with those economists who — now — say that if anything has been relearned in recent years, it is that laissez faire does not work in banking and for institution-building in general.[1] This is true. But the second generation reforms will be less radical, less visible, less headline-creating, less ideological, much slower and much more influenced by lobbying and rent-seeking, etc. It will be, therefore, connected with a serious danger which did not exist at the beginning: institution-building and regulatory processes may be used for the creeping change of the whole system from a free society to interventionism and neocorporativism. It is our task to prevent it.

Comments on Capital Markets and Their Size, Structure and Regulation

Introductory comments at the first annual Conference on Capital Markets: Effects of Regulation on Economic Growth, Prague, May 6, 1997

It is a great pleasure to be here this morning, to welcome all of you to Prague and to discuss one of the new, very recent institutions of our economy: capital markets. I am also honored to introduce our special guest and distinguished speaker, Joseph Stiglitz.

While preparing myself for this meeting, I picked up a small booklet with the title "Financial Systems for Eastern Europe's Emerging Democracies" written by Joseph Stiglitz in 1993, which was based on his earlier talk in Prague.[2]

I agree with him that "well-functioning capital markets are at the heart of a well-functioning capitalist economy."[3] I also agree that "of all the markets in the economy, the capital markets are perhaps the most complicated and least understood." And finally, I agree that "the structure of capital markets appears vastly different among major capitalist economies," which makes it practically impossible to translate one simple piece of legislation in one country and implement it in another.

There is no doubt that capital markets are different from ordinary markets and that they need more government intervention or regulation than ordinary markets. The only question is how to intervene, how to regulate them without constraining them unnecessarily and without expecting too much from the regulator, who is a human being like the rest of us, with his well-defined utility function which he tries to maximize, and who operates in a world of intensive rent-seeking and the well-known fallacies of regulation. I am not very optimistic about regulation in general and about regulation of capital markets in particular.

Let me say a few words about the whole issue as I see it.

1. In the last couple of years our capital market has grown much faster than anyone expected. It is easy to criticize our expectations with the benefit of hindsight, but it happened and I would dare to argue that we were not alone in making the same or a similar forecasting mistake. We know that we gave it a strong accelerating impulse by our voucher privatization but — again — I expected a much slower beginning.

2. I have to confess that in the early '90s, at the moment when the whole economy was being liberalized, I fully shared Joseph Stiglitz's view that "to a large extent, equity markets are an interesting and amusing sideshow, but they are not at the heart of the action."[4] I expected that banks would play a dominant role in raising funds and in the allocation of capital for some non-negligible time to come. Even now this remains true from the quantitative point of view here, but we understood that the capital markets play a role which is much bigger than their pure size.
3. We, therefore, started our economic transformation with heavy reliance on the banking system. While trying to expand rapidly the totally undeveloped or almost nonexistent banking system, we probably underestimated the importance of imposing sufficiently high capital requirements (which is what Joseph Stiglitz strongly recommends in his booklet) and at the same time we did not succeed in strictly dividing the financial and production sectors of the economy. We more or less accepted the German (or continental) type of banking with its strong interrelationships between banks and firms in the production sector. We see many problems with it now. I did not want it even then, but I am not sure we could have started differently.
4. I am aware of the fact that with the spontaneous evolution of our financial markets, with literally millions of shareholders and hundreds of investment companies and funds, mostly as a result of voucher privatization, we did not succeed in helping to create one important public good, which is the sufficient degree of information about the financial position of firms. It is partly the result of the lack of intensity of transactions in today's markets, which is unavoidable (the markets are shallow and, therefore, not sufficiently efficient), and it may be at the same time the result of some delayed legislative measures on the side of the government. The question of lags in public policy is, however, not simple. Joseph Stiglitz, as a well-known expert in the field of the economics of information, mentioned in his study that "much of the return in capital markets consists of rent-seeking," and I have to admit that in the past some of us did not immediately believe all the critics of our capital markets because they usually played their own card and did not take sufficiently into consideration the existing stage in the evolution of our economic systems.[5] Their criticism was very often indistinguishable from the complaints of those who just incurred a loss by making a wrong investment.

5. As you know, the Czech government recently introduced the so-called "package of measures." If I put aside its macroeconomic side, one of its main intentions is to make our financial markets more transparent and more standard. By declaring such an intention, we wanted to send a strong signal both to domestic and foreign investors.

The main institutional change of this policy package as far as the capital markets are concerned is the creation of an independent Securities and Exchange Commission. We hope that it will be interpreted positively by investors and we will try to have it managed by a respected team of professionals. As an economist, I know that the term "independence" has its own problems, but we will try to avoid the interference of various vested interests among capital market participants.

The second field of change concerns the problems that currently exist through excessive concentration of ownership in the hands of our major banks. The respective authorities were given three months to analyze the situation and prepare legislation which would eliminate the worst aspects of this concentration and allow for gradual divestiture by the banks of their fund management subsidiaries. We will also prepare an amendment to the existing laws which would eliminate share ownership in the investment funds by fund managers and would also ban the funds from dealing with related parties of the fund manager.

The economic package further strengthens the role of depository banks (custodians) to the investment funds. Negligence in this area will be dealt with very strictly and will mean losing the license for this service. There are many other suggestions but it is not my ambition to go into details here.

We know as well that the main problem is not the legislation itself; it is becoming more and more standard. The problem is law enforcement and sufficient control and regulation. There is a clear need to speed up judicial procedures and to establish specialized financial courts to deal with bankruptcies and matters related to capital markets.

Finally, I would like to make a short remark concerning foreign investors. Some of them have invested in the investment funds which were created during the first and the second wave of voucher privatization. The dominant feature of that procedure was substantial discounts to the net asset value of the funds. In some cases the discounts reached 70 percent to 80 percent. To a discriminating investor this would clearly indicate a specific risk which the market placed on such an investment. Regardless of this "warning," they bought into these funds and now are crying for help. We were inexperienced and innocent; they should not have been.

Nevertheless, I believe we have left the first, kindergarten stage behind us and from now on the situation will be different. For investors, their lives will be in some respects easier, in other respects they will be more difficult, because more standard.

Emerging Markets and Their Current Problems: The Czech Perspective

Notes for lecture at the Delhi School of Economics, New Delhi, March 11, 1999

We are quickly approaching the end of one of the most promising decades of the 20th century. The decade started with many hopes, which were connected to the collapse of communism, to the softening, if not the elimination, of East-West tensions, and to an apparent takeoff of some developing countries which succeeded in breaking the vicious circle of poverty and underdevelopment.

I do not know whether the same feeling was dominant here in India as well, but in my country, in the Czech Republic, we were at that time convinced of the coming of a new world. Everyone foresaw the era of freedom, of democracy, of openness, the era of true independence, the era of the possibility of fulfilling all personal dreams, desires and goals, which were blocked in the communist regime. Coming from Central (or perhaps Eastern) Europe, I can assure you that the same atmosphere prevailed in the whole, suddenly liberated part of Europe. My trips to Southeast Asia and Latin America convinced me that the same atmosphere existed in those regions as well.

The feelings at the end of the 1990s are definitely different and not so optimistic in spite of the fact that the countries in question underwent a rapid transition. They liberalized, deregulated and privatized their economies and societies (and my country was very radical in this respect) and as a result, central planning and bureaucratic administration of the economies ceased to exist. Markets emerged, but I do not dare to argue that deep, strong and really efficient markets have been created in less than a decade. Liberalization and deregulation are necessary but insufficient preconditions. The markets have to evolve. They cannot be created by decree, by law or by regulation. We have to admit that the existing markets are still shallow, weak and, therefore, not fully efficient and that they are vulnerable to the whole variety of external or internal shocks. This is truer, the more the countries have liberalized, deregulated and opened their markets to the rest of the world.

The liberal, market-oriented reforms created enormous expectations. The complexities and difficulties of the transition were — at least rhetorically — recognized, but almost everyone assumed that the elimination of the past irrational system would bring about tangible results in a relatively short period of time. This feeling was probably stronger in the Czech Republic than elsewhere in the region, because 60 years ago, before the communist takeover, the country was among the most industrialized countries in the world. I know something about the attempts in India to industrialize the economy in the '50s and '60s and about Prof. Mahalanobis' planning ambitions, but we were in a much different position. We industrialized an already industrialized country which was a unique — and, of course, unsuccessful — experiment. It led to a drastic deindustrialization after the collapse of communism and its sheltered markets, and to the quick return to a more or less normal, harmonic economic structure, but at the cost of large-scale dislocations and disruptions.

Most of us understood that the time scale required for the rebirth of a full-fledged market economy, together with the establishment of all corresponding institutions of market infrastructure, is much longer than was originally assumed and especially much longer than people wanted to wait. Because of that, the e-r gap (as I used to call the expectations-reality gap), is getting bigger, not smaller.[6]

I am sure you went through a very similar experience. It does not mean (or imply), however, that the market-oriented reforms should be interrupted or reversed. On the contrary, I am deeply convinced that they have no alternative and — even with the benefit of hindsight — I believe in my "Ten Commandments of Systemic Reform," which I put together in 1993 and which influenced on the one hand and reflected on the other the Czech economic transformation.[7]

As I said, the end of 1990s brought about the undeniable loss of a more or less general (or at least overwhelming) consensus both about the structure of the transformation strategy and the interpretation of transformation achievements. We should not panic, we should not accept cheap and oversimplified headlines in the media, we should pay more attention to the empirical data than to the political slogans used in the election campaign and we should especially not become victims of the vested interests of a very skillfully organized group of international advisers, investment bankers, powerful auditors and bureaucrats of international financial organizations. They established a very successful rent-seeking and pressure group.

To my great regret, the Czech economy is currently undergoing a severe depression, which was initiated by a policy mistake in the middle of 1996. The rapid economic growth between 1993 and 1996 (which in 1995 reached 6.4 percent) was accompanied by a typical external imbalance (growing imports led to the current account deficit of about 7 percent of GDP) and it provoked the Central Bank to dramatically slow down the money supply growth and to introduce other restrictive measures. The standard sequence of events evolved together with an avalanche of deteriorating confidence and we are currently in a deep credit crunch which is very difficult to overcome.

I am convinced that our case does not represent an accidental or isolated event. It is part of a more general framework which I want to briefly discuss.

We are witnessing a visible increase in instability (both economic and political) in the transition countries of Asia, Latin America and Europe. We know as well that its costs are very high and that they are paid by the affected countries themselves, not by anyone else. They are, therefore, highly motivated to look for its explanation and solution, more than the international financial institutions.

The first task is to find out what happened and why it happened. We should be able to answer such a simple question as "why did it not happen in all transition economies?" There must be some important characteristics existing in the affected countries and that does not existing in unaffected countries.

I mentioned countries of three continents, and did not mention the fourth continent, Africa. This may be important. It seems to me that Africa was not affected because in recent years the continent did not experience huge capital inflows, which can practically overnight change sign and become capital outflows. Similar differences can be found among countries inside continents. *The more the country was considered to be a success (realized or promised), the more open and more deregulated it was, the more vulnerable to crisis it was and the more often the crisis really happened.* Saying that, I do not want to suggest that there is a direct causal relationship between capital inflows and financial crises. I prefer to consider huge capital inflows to be a fertile land for a future crisis. And I would like to stress that I do not use this argument as a basis for the now fashionable idea that the flow of capital between countries should be limited or restricted.

Recently, a new, powerful and politically interesting explanation came to the fore. The affected countries themselves have been blamed for their political and economic immaturity, for the imperfection of their financial and banking systems, for their lack of capital market supervision, for their incompleteness of property rights reforms, etc. This explanation is in my opinion based on a misunderstanding of the transition process and its peculiarities, and more on anecdotal evidence than on hard data, and it seems to me that the well-known imperfections cannot explain the degree of instability and the severity of the recession.

I cannot buy this interpretation easily for a very simple reason. The whole decade of the '90s was in all of these countries devoted to the institutional (sometimes called "structural" in International Monetary Fund jargon) transformation, and even if its relative success was very uneven, there is no doubt that the degree of immaturity or imperfection of those economies is much less in 1999 than it was in 1990. Therefore, something else had to happen and I am afraid it did happen.

The countries exporting capital (or perhaps individual economic agents in those countries) misinterpreted the economic preparedness (and health) of countries eager to import capital and sent more capital there than was appropriate. In addition, they (together with the IMF and World Bank) convinced the importing countries that the outflows of capital must have the same easiness as the inflows. An atmosphere was created where anyone who dared to raise simple questions about the rationality of such arrangements was caricatured as an antiliberal advocate of mercantilism or of inward-looking economic policies.

Such an arrangement, where some were more equal than others (in a true Orwellian sense), which was supplemented by the quasi-patronage of the IMF and the moral hazard connected therewith, put all the good cards into the hands of capital-exporting countries and placed all the risks on capital-importing countries. It was not accepted that investors seeking higher returns in emerging markets than in developed countries must accept higher risks as well. On the contrary, the lenders could rely on being rescued — at least since the Mexico crisis in 1980. This was because capital investment was hypocritically interpreted as a help, as foreign assistance. I remember how often I warned foreign investors who wanted to help us and asked them to make a good business decision, not provide charity. The problem was reinforced by IMF´s interventions based on a traditional bureaucratic incentive to be involved. The IMF simply could not or did not want to let countries reform on their own, since doing so would undermine the organization's significance.

The problem was aggravated by the way in which the emerging-markets crisis was handled once it had developed. I agree with Jeffrey Sachs, Rudiger Dornbusch, John Makin, Martin Feldstein and many others who speak about the mishandling of the crisis. The IMF and its influence-respecting central banks in the affected countries did not distinguish the fatal difference between the inflationary and deflationary worlds, did not shift their policies in due time from fighting inflation (and external imbalance) to averting recession, did not understand that the scarce commodity may be demand, not supply, and that the dogmatic denial of the credit problem and the prolonged continuation of restrictive policies may lead to economic suicide.

The IMF wanted to keep capital in the affected country by all means, especially by extremely high interest rates. Waiting for the magic return of confidence with high interest rates and with no new credit to domestic firms, however, did not work. It caused severe recessions and financial distress. As a result, even healthy banks and companies collapsed, even the best-managed firms were driven into bankruptcy, and loans that were originally good rapidly turned into bad ones. Nevertheless, the affected countries were constantly blamed for their weak banks, bad loans, lack of financial supervision and their imperfect capital markets, and it was forgotten that in a deflationary situation even the best economies have similar problems.

I started my speech by stressing the importance of the fall of communism. But this historic moment did not end the great debates of this century. It began a new one, or, perhaps, should have. The debate we need now is between individualism and statism, between responsibility and free-riding, between liberty and social consciousness. It should have taken place much earlier in this century, but — at least in my part of the world — communism distracted us. We have to use the chance we have now.

What Lessons Can Be Learned from Privatization in a Post-Communist Country: The Czech Experience

Notes for statement in the session "Building International Consensus and Defining Models for Privatization" at the seventh annual World Economic Development Congress, Washington, D.C., September 30, 1998

It is a great pleasure and a great honor to be again, after six years, at the World Economic Development Congress.

I accepted the title of this session, and I accept that I am supposed to talk about "international consensus" and "models for privatization." It seems to me that, after the past decade of privatization and radical economic transformation, we are still in need of an international consensus. I will try to say a few words about it.

There is — at least I hope — a basic consensus regarding the *positive* effects of privatization, which has become considered, together with liberalization and deregulation, the crucial way for creating a free, open, transparent and more efficient economy. The last decade of the 20th century was in this respect a decisive breakthrough. Now, practically all governments in the world talk about privatization, even if it does not necessarily mean that they follow through with it. But the idea of privatization is here and I am convinced that it is here to stay.

There is, however, much less consensus about the scope and speed of privatization. As a result, the ideological disputes (on one hand) and the rent-seeking activities (on the other) are these days not about privatization as much as they are about its scope and speed. The disagreements, however, are no less important or less dangerous. There are, and there will always be, strong vested interests (both theoretical and practical, purely "idealistic" as well as "materialistic") against large-scale and fast privatization. We should be aware of them and should not, therefore, weaken or soften our effort to privatize as much and as fast as possible. We should not forget or conceal the fact that privatization — like any other human activity — has its costs and benefits, but we should keep arguing that its long-term benefits are much bigger than its short-term costs. Because of those nonzero costs, the purely ideological arguments in favor of privatization may not be sufficient. Serious economic arguments must follow.

Privatization does not take place in a vacuum. Because of that, *privatization methods* depend on the scope and speed of privatization and its scope and speed depend on *the size of the privatization task.* We have to start there.

The size of the privatization task is relatively small in a developed Western country, as in a typical economy of Western Europe. The privatization is done there at the margin of the economy. (It does not imply, however, that the task is simple and easy or that its benefits are only marginal.) In such a country the privatization is done inside a full-fledged market economy, with functioning capital markets and all the other institutions of a market economy. Another important characteristic of such an economy is the existence of domestic capital which can compete with foreign capital. In this situation, the speed is not crucial and the privatization methods should be, therefore, standard ones (described in elementary textbooks).

The size of the privatization task is totally different in a former communist country, where private property was fully (or mostly) eliminated by full-scale nationalization. The privatization is done there at the heart of the economy or, to put it differently, *with the whole economy*. You do not privatize individual firms but the economy as a whole. The privatization is done in a rudimentary market economy, in an economy without efficiently functioning capital markets and with only simultaneously arising accompanying institutions of market infrastructure. After decades of communist rule, domestic capital does not exist and there is no one to compete with foreign capital. In this situation, in the dangerous moment of preprivatization chaos and "agony," speed is crucial and the privatization methods should be a mixture of standard and non-standard ones. The Czech so-called voucher-privatization was probably the most innovative idea in this respect.

I am deeply convinced that international consensus should be built around this concept, around the understanding of *the difference between classical and non-classical, small-scale and large-scale, marginal and fundamental, efficiency-enhancing (in individual cases) and system-changing privatization.*

I am afraid that such a consensus does not yet exist. The concept of privatization was originally erroneously transferred from one institutional setting to another; the importance of alternative methods was neither understood nor accepted; and prolongation of the preprivatization era (because of the insistence on standard, slow methods) was recommended to the detriment of all.

It would have been extremely helpful to have achieved such a consensus a decade ago. Many of the former communist countries have, in the meantime, moved to another stage of their development and the property structure of their economies is much different. Privatization occurs already at the margin; it is less wholesale, it is more individual. The two models I suggested have become nowadays — I hope — more important for the interpretation of the events of the last decade (and of their consequences) than for future privatizations. To understand them is, nevertheless, very important.[8]

Promoting Financial Stability in the Transition Economies of Central and Eastern Europe

Address at the 21st annual Economic Symposium on Policy Issues, Federal Reserve Bank of Kansas City, Jackson Hole, Wyoming, August 29, 1997

It is a great pleasure to be here after seven years, to have the chance to meet old friends and to report on the non-negligible and undeniably positive results which have been achieved in the transition economies of Central and Eastern Europe between my two visits to Jackson Hole, and also about the undeniable problems that emerged in this unique historical maneuver. The seven-year time span makes it possible to base our discussion on the existence and understanding of many important similarities among the transforming countries which are, however, sometimes difficult to discover behind evident differences. I will use mostly Czech data and Czech experience, but my ambition is to at least implicitly generalize and outline broader tendencies or principles.

I happened to be here in 1990, at a time of optimistic forecasts and expectations and of preparations for radical moves forward in the near future. As we see it now, the future was not identical for all the countries in question. It is not difficult to say why. Some countries spent that critical period in unproductive political debates without the ability to formulate clear visions and transformation strategies. Because of that, they made costly concessions to all, loosened fiscal and monetary controls, intensified economic imbalances inherited from the communist past, and further destabilized the economy as a whole. It could have been expected that to liberalize prices and foreign trade in such an unstable situation meant to bring about rapid and persistent inflation, sharp economic decline, huge shifts in income and wealth distribution as well as the deterioration of living conditions of large segments of the population. As a consequence, the vital reform measures were blocked or postponed to a much less favorable situation.

Other countries, however, used the preparatory stage for generating essential preconditions for the implementation of subsequent radical reforms. When I was here in 1990, my talk was mostly devoted to the discussion of these preconditions.[9] I stressed the importance of restrictive macroeconomic policies, e.g., cautious monetary policies and surplus state budgets, as the only way to avoid falling into what I used to call the "reform trap."

History proved that the implementation of such a restrictive macro policy, together with merciless devaluation, made the opening of domestic and foreign markets possible at relatively low costs to society. I will briefly discuss the situation in both the internal and external sphere in the last years as an argument in this respect.

The rate of inflation after price liberalization in my country moved very rapidly to a more or less acceptable level, as can be seen from the following table (price liberalization was carried out on January 1, 1991):

Month of 1991	1	2	3	4	5	6	7	8	9	10
Rate of Inflation (month to month) in %	25.8	6.1	4.3	2.4	1.9	1.8	-0.3	0.0	0.3	0.2

I agree with those economists who argue that to reduce it further and faster would have been very costly. With the exception of the deliberate price shift in January 1993 (as a result of the introduction of the value-added tax system), the seasonally adjusted monthly inflation did not exceed the 1 percent level very often and was always below 2 percent. (The synergistic effect of currency depreciation, of a radical shift in deregulation of rent and energy prices, and of floods in July 1997 is, however, a different story.)

The annual rate of inflation since 1992 has been rather stubborn at about the 10 percent level, with the lowest annual rate achieved this April at 6.3 percent. The relative persistence of such an inflation rate cannot in my view be explained by monetary or macroeconomic factors only or predominantly, because there were important structural factors (and impulses) at play, connected with the extraordinarily high frequency of changes in relative prices. It was an integral and necessary part of the restructuring of both nominal and real variables in the transforming economy.

My conclusion is that the inflation slowdown to such a moderate level could have been achieved, provided cautious macroeconomic policies were pursued with sufficient consistency.

It was more difficult to achieve external equilibrium. *In the first stage, in the moment of substantial economic decline* (1991-1993) — which was caused by an unavoidable transformation-shakeout of nonviable economic activities associated with the old economic system, not by excessive macroeconomic restrictions (as was sometimes suggested) — domestic aggregate demand did not reach the level of the aggregate supply. There was, evidently, a shortage of domestic demand. As a result, exports were bigger than imports which, together with strong capital inflows, preserved a balance of payments equilibrium and led to the growing stock of hard currency reserves.

In the second stage, in the moment of economic recovery (1994-1996), rapid growth of investment (and a very high investment ratio, exceeding significantly the domestic saving ratio), together with our rather innocent opening of the whole economy toward more protected trade partners, produced a radically different outcome. The aggregate demand exceeded the domestic aggregate supply and imports exceeded exports. At first, the balance of trade, then the current account of the balance of payments and finally the capital account turned into deficit. As is well-known, the final stage of the drama was played by massive speculation against the Czech crown in May 1997, by its unintended depreciation and by its free floating since that time.

This recent accident was undoubtedly the most important phenomenon of instability in our whole post-communist era, of financial instability in a broader sense. We have to admit that we did not succeed in finding an easy and straightforward way to prevent it.

Was it possible to avoid it at all? It is too early to give a final answer but I have some reservations about it, given all the political and economic domestic and international constraints, and will therefore try here, today, to briefly discuss some relevant arguments in this respect as I see them.

1. The exchange rate regime and the exchange rate level

The collapse of communism "happened" at the moment when the economics profession believed in fixed exchange rates and in the advantage of anchoring the economy by means of one fixed point – especially in a situation when all other variables undergo large changes and fluctuations. I have to confess that I was originally afraid of introducing such a rigid regime, but the first impressions were positive because we succeeded in choosing an exchange rate which functioned well for 76 months. By sufficiently devaluating the crown on the eve of price liberalization, we formed something that I later called the "transformation cushion." The exchange rate cushion (as well as the parallel wage cushion) appeared to be crucial for the whole subsequent transformation process. The inflation differential was not as big in our case as in some other transforming countries, but the appreciation in real terms reached almost 80 percent in 76 months, which was too much. Although we have been constantly checking the remaining thickness of our exchange rate cushion, as we see it now, probably in the middle of 1996 we missed the most suitable moment for the abolition of the fixed exchange rate regime. The question is, however, whether the subsequent movements of the rate of exchange would have been less dramatic than they were in reality in recent months. The vulnerability of an emerging market economy is in this respect very high and, probably, unavoidable.

Tentative lesson No. 1: A fixed exchange rate regime should not last too long.

2. Investment-savings imbalance

Since 1993, the economic recovery has been relatively rapid (in European terms). It was pulled by strong investment demand (with only modestly growing private consumption and exports, and with stagnating or declining government expenditures).

The rapid growth of investments seems to be unavoidable. The problem is in the structure of investments. The overwhelming feeling of obsolescence of infrastructure (of all kinds) after four decades of communism, together with overambitious "green" attempts to rapidly undo the well-documented environmental damage caused by the absence of private property and a market economy, led to an extremely high investment ratio (33 percent in 1996). Only a smaller part of investment was "productive" in the narrow sense and contributed to industrial restructuring and modernization. To reconcile strong investment demand with domestic savings was almost impossible, because we did not succeed in creating the atmosphere of "belt-tightening" as the only way to overcome the heavy burden of the communist heritage. The problem is clear, the solution not.

Tentative lesson No. 2: It is necessary to restrain ambitions to "catch-up" and the impatience of society as much as possible.

3. Wage-Productivity Nexus and the Degree of Competitiveness

Price liberalization, accompanied by a rather restrictive macroeconomic policy, generated another significant transformation phenomenon: the wage cushion, because wages went up much slower than prices. As a result, real wages could for some time grow faster than GDP or productivity without undermining the competitiveness of the whole economy. It gave our enterprise sector breathing space, which only a part of it effectively used for radical restructuring. We were, however, not able to prolong the process of emptying the cushion. The government could not control the private sector and was not able (or strong enough) to block the growth of salaries and wages in the public sector. The relatively rapid growth of wages in the private sector was made possible by the soft (or insufficiently hard) granting of credit by the banking sector and by the slow process of bankruptcies on the one hand and strong demand for labor and very low unemployment on the other. None of these factors could be directly controlled by the government.

Tentative lesson No. 3: The rate of growth of wages is not a "free" policy variable (as is sometimes implicitly suggested by external observers and advisers).

4. Quality of Markets, Economic Strength and High Degree of Foreign Trade Liberalization

With the benefit of hindsight, it can be argued that the scope and rapidity with which former communist countries opened their economies and adopted currency convertibility was much larger and faster than in similar historical moments in the past. As we all know, it took a much longer time to do in Western Europe and Japan after the war. And, in addition, it was done in a situation with a high degree of globalization of world markets and in a situation with enormous structural shifts in the financial system itself, as well as in a moment of sophisticated protectionism in developed countries (in Europe especially). We do not know whether it was a blessing or a curse. The entry of strong firms from developed countries into our unprotected markets was much easier than the entry of our technologically, financially and organizationally much weaker firms into their "occupied" and protected markets. When I say that, I do not mean it as an advocacy of the policy of sheltering the markets of young, immature industries. I use it, however, as a part of my explanation of our trade deficit.

Tentative lesson No. 4: A small, open, industrial ex-communist economy pays more for trade and currency liberalization in the short run than a big, less open and less industrial economy.

5. Fiscal and Monetary Policy Mix

Until very recently, we succeeded in having either surplus or balanced budgets and a relatively cautious monetary policy (with unknown shifts in the velocity of money).[10]

It seems natural to argue that the growing external imbalance required some degree of macroeconomic tightening. But the politicians had the feeling that to have budgets without deficits for seven consecutive years was the maximum they could offer. To criticize them in this respect seems to me inappropriate.

Some degree of money supply deceleration was necessary as well. It did happen in our case, but to slow down the annual rate of money supply growth from 18 to 20 percent (in the first half of 1996) to 10 to 12 percent (in the second half of 1996) and to 6 to 7 percent (in the first half of 1997) by an unannounced step of the Central Bank was something which at least asks for a discussion of the real meaning of central bank independence. It had, as expected, a faster impact upon aggregate supply than demand and contributed to the apparent economic slowdown (if not decline), to unexpected budgetary problems (on the income side), to heavy political conflict and uncertainty and, finally, to increased financial instability as well as to the recent currency weakness.

Tentative lesson No. 5: To make sharp changes in monetary policy proves to be very dangerous.

6. Fragility of Financial Institutions

Financial institutions (banks and other financial intermediaries) in the post-communist countries have many "childhood" problems and cannot be relied upon to contribute sufficiently to the stability of the whole economy. Whether we wanted it or not, the banks and other financial institutions were an integral part of the transformation process and could not get the status of a "clean" outsider as was sometimes suggested. They inherited difficult loan portfolios; with their involvement in transformation and privatizations they added assets that were not much less controversial. They have complicated ownership structures, etc. The masterminding of their evolution is, however, impossible.

There is no doubt that the fragility of our financial markets was an additional complicating factor. Their lack of transparency and stability contributed to the slowdown of capital inflows and aggravated the balance of payments problem. The only relevant question is what could have been done *ex ante*.

Capital markets are different from ordinary markets and they probably need more government intervention or regulation. The problem is how to intervene, how to regulate them without constraining them unnecessarily and without expecting too much from the regulator, who is a human being like the rest of us (with his well-defined utility function which he tries to maximize) and who operates in a world of intensive rent-seeking and in a world of the well-known fallacies of regulation. I am not very optimistic about regulation in general and about regulation of capital markets in particular.[11]

Our capital market has grown much faster than anyone expected, especially when we gave it a strong accelerating impulse by our voucher privatization. In the early '90s I fully shared Joseph Stiglitz's view that "to a large extent, equity markets are an interesting and amusing sideshow, but they are not at the heart of the action" because we started our economic transformation with a heavy reliance on the banking system.[12] While trying to expand it rapidly, we probably underestimated the need to impose sufficiently high capital requirements and, at the same time, did not succeed in strictly dividing the financial and production sectors of the economy. We more or less accepted the German (or continental) type of banking with its strong interrelationships between banks and firms in the production sector. We see many problems with it now, but I am not sure we could have started differently.

With the spontaneous evolution of our financial markets, with literally millions of shareholders and hundreds of investment companies and funds, mostly as a byproduct of voucher privatization, we failed to generate a sufficient degree of information about the financial position of individual firms. It is connected with the lack of intensity of transactions in today's markets, which is unavoidable (the markets are shallow and, therefore, not efficient), and it may be at the same time the result of delayed legislative measures by the government.

The question of lags in public policy is, however, not simple. Joseph Stiglitz mentioned in his study that "much of the return in capital markets consists of rent-seeking" and I have to admit that in the past some of us did not immediately believe all the critics of our capital markets because they usually played their own card and did not take into consideration the existing stage of the evolution of the whole economic system.[13] Their criticism was very often indistinguishable from the complaints of those who just incurred a loss by making a wrong investment.

The main problem is not the legislation itself. The problem is law enforcement, efficient control and rational regulation. There is a clear need to speed up judicial procedures and to establish specialized financial courts dealing with bankruptcies and matters related to capital markets.

Tentative lesson No. 6: The capital markets begin to function faster than you expect and before you try to regulate them.

To conclude, I have to repeat that my answers to the existing problems are tentative, but I hope that they clearly suggest that my doubts about the possibility of a smooth and stable transition path in politically and socially difficult, but highly democratic, pluralistic and open economies and societies of Central and Eastern Europe continue to exist because we are not in a "brave new world" of perfect markets and of perfect governments. It remains our task, however, to minimize the inevitable instability.

Three Years after the Currency Crisis

SVU Congress, Washington, D.C. August 10, 2000

Three years have passed since the biggest economic disturbance of the post-communist era in one country. I said the biggest and, with the hindsight of three years and the knowledge of economic statistics for that period as well as for the period that followed, I dare say that the events of that period constituted a political rather than an economic crisis.

I shall therefore discuss:

- What happened before the crisis?
- What occurred between the first deliberate macroeconomic restrictive intervention and the beginning of a currency crisis?
- What happened during the crisis itself?
- What happened when the most acute crisis was over?

I. The anatomy of our currency crisis

I distinguish between four basic periods which have a number of different characteristics:

(a) Before the crisis, in 1994 and 1995 and during the first half of 1996, the Czech Republic experienced a relatively high rate of economic growth, and in 1995 its GDP reached an almost unbelievable year-on-year growth rate of 6.4 percent.

This was a "classical" transformation recovery.

Given the very low rate of unemployment (which throughout most of this period did not exceed 3 percent), the fact that inflation was not falling (its annual rate remained at roughly 10 percent, in those days considerably less than in other economies undergoing transformation) was not a cause for concern or for a change of policy. Neither were we concerned with the country's fiscal situation because throughout this period we achieved balanced budgets. It is true that some economists, including influential official institutions like the Czech National Bank and the IMF were critical of some phenomena but their main concern was the supposed rapid growth of wages. I would therefore argue that in those days the growth of wages was unacceptable only to those who wanted to achieve, in a relatively short time, a drastic reduction in inflation.

For those of us who, on the contrary, considered such a sharp drop in inflation to be extremely dangerous and irresponsible because we were aware — given that expectations concerning the development of nominal variables remained unchanged — that this would dramatically endanger economic growth, the growth in average earnings in itself was not a serious problem.

For six years, since the last days of December 1990, the nominal rate of exchange had been totally stable, even though the actual rate, due to the inflation differential, was visibly rising. This resulted in the gradual emptying of another transformation cushion, and the only question was how full or how empty this cushion was at any given time. No big change in this respect occurred even after October 2, 1995, when the crown officially became a fully convertible currency. A more significant change occurred in February 1996, when the crown's fluctuation band was widened to 7.5 percent in both directions, which did mark a change in the exchange policy but, as became clear later, not an adequate one. This became evident throughout the following year, 1996, when the position of the crown continued to strengthen, for instance, against the German mark from 18.45 crowns (for 1 DM) in February to 17.63 in December.

It is also worth pointing out that in November 1995, Standard & Poor's granted the Czech Republic, as the first post-communist country, the rating "A" and that in December the Czech Republic — again as the first — became a full member of the OECD.

However, tensions in the economy continued to grow. Even then, the authorities were not denying it. The main problem was the very high level of investment (considerably exceeding domestic savings) which was, moreover, in addition to environmental and infrastructural investments, directed chiefly towards the tertiary sector, so that a relatively small proportion of funds remained available for modernizing industry. The total amount of investments was not identical to their ability to create new capacities. Let us also mention the fact that in those days this high level of investment was generally praised (not criticized) and that the government was not able to intervene in order to change the structure of investment. Nor can I remember anybody systematically criticizing such a rate of investment. Representatives of the Czech National Bank who attended all government meetings did not put forward a single important proposal. No one tried to reduce the rate of investment and neither did the debate on earnings explicitly aim at that, even though it could be said that implicitly it was concerned with the ratio between consumption and savings.

The imbalance between savings and investment was mirrored in the external imbalance as demonstrated by the deficit in the trade balance and the current-account balance which occurred more or less irrespective of the rate of exchange, or which a slight alteration of the rate of exchange would not have significantly affected. Only when this internal imbalance was seen to "spill over" into the external imbalance, as happened during 1996, did it begin to be taken seriously. The balance of payments turned out to be the most worrying issue of the economy. However, as long as the country remained politically stable, retained its high creditworthiness abroad and thus also a sufficient flow of foreign investment, the current-account deficit was not thought to pose an immediate problem.

Many of us realized even then that this was an extremely dangerous situation which could change rapidly and unexpectedly. We knew how suddenly such a crisis could develop, as was demonstrated by the example of Mexico, which was for us a serious warning. We were definitely not being naïve and unconcerned.

We knew quite well how easily the political situation could change, both at home and abroad, and how unexpectedly the economy could suffer an unpleasant exogenous shock. We knew that investors were capable of panicking on the basis of quite innocuous impulses, leading to a domino or avalanche effect, and that the economy could also find itself in difficulties due to its own, i.e., endogenous, processes, etc., etc. We also knew that in real life one was more likely to encounter a combination of all of these aspects, which can augment each other, and that it was therefore extremely important to discourage their mutual synergy by all means available to domestic economic policy.

Another point worth making is the relatively unfavorable structure of foreign investment which was caused, apart from the general character and fundamental logic of our transformation, by the manner in which our economy was opened up to the outside world (above all in the financial sphere). The key moment in this opening up to the world was October 1995 — before we had entered the OECD — when financial flows were liberalized even in the balance-of-payments capital account. The Czech Republic thus had become unique among all the transition economies. The crown began to be widely traded on international money markets, resulting in tens of billions of euro crowns outside the control of our central bank. Nothing similar to that existed then, or exists now, in the case, for instance, of the forint or the zloty, not to mention other currencies. This premature opening up of the capital account, which made me feel very uneasy then, was motivated — apart from reasons of prestige — by the efforts of the Czech National Bank (CNB) to bring down the cost of sterilizing the flow of speculative capital into the country but, it must be said, the desired effect did not occur. Quite the opposite, the doors were opened wide, enabling rapid movements of speculative capital, unfortunately in both directions.

A rational look at our situation should have led to attempts to start carefully slowing down the economy. This would have reduced the existing tensions, but not disrupted the economy. Domestic and foreign investors would not have become alarmed, our banking and financial system would not have been endangered and the Czech way of economic transformation would not have been discredited. It is clear that measures to slow down the economy should have ideally been taken already in the middle of 1995, but for a number of reasons this did not happen. The government had little desire to start slowing down the economy in the runup to the elections.

(b) It was in this complicated economic situation that parliamentary elections were held in June 1996 and their result — rather surprisingly — failed to confirm the previous position of the parties in the governing coalition. The complicated coalition negotiations which followed resulted in a very unstable minority government (made possible by the consent of the Social Democrats, but without any firm basis such as an opposition agreement). The government's space for maneuvering was thus further curtailed. I hope people have not forgotten these facts. The weakness of the government was exploited by forces both at home and abroad for a fundamental attack on the "Czech way of transformation." The Czech economy fell to the political ambitions of some segments of the Czech political scene, rather than being a victim of its own imperfections.

Given the circumstances, the most important thing was not to make mistakes and to ensure that the government and the central bank did not create unnecessary disturbances. Unfortunately this did not happen. On June 19, before coalition negotiations on setting up a new government were concluded, and without any consultation with the existing, "old" outgoing government, the central bank announced strict restrictive measures. It is clear that it wanted to slow down the economy and that this step was taken deliberately. However, the central bank did not know to what extent this measure would be effective. It considerably raised minimum reserve requirements (from 8.5 to 11.5 percent) and at the same time interbank interest rates (bank rate, Lombard rate and repo rate). Our weak banks, with their inadequate capital resources, many of them in a very precarious position for a number of easily explained reasons and at the limit of their possibilities, were affected by this intervention much more than our central bank anticipated or took into consideration even afterwards. Commercial banks were obliged to withdraw billions of crowns from circulation by August 9. Unless there is no idle money, such a measure is not and cannot be easy, painless and without consequences. Some banks failed to cope and soon ceased to exist. Others survived but paid a price in the form of enormous problems in the future and of disturbing the fragile balance of the corporate sphere, where attempts to cope with the bank's intervention led to mass cancellation of credit or refusal to extend existing credit. The relatively well known statistics on the amount of money in circulation and on newly proffered credit amply support this conclusion.

I would like to suggest that it was precisely at this point that the direct route to the currency crisis began. First came a very unpleasant signal — the collapse of the First Credit and Loan Bank in Pilsen. Shortly afterwards the CNB clashed with our biggest private bank, Agrobanka, which was later practically forced into liquidation. (There is still no proper explanation of the events because the versions that were put forward by Agrobanka and the CNB differed substantially and still do.)

The government failed to react decisively and convincingly, but without the cooperation of the CNB it could hardly have been possible. The government had problems of its own, particularly with the preparation of the budget for 1997, and the budget debate in a split Parliament considerably destabilized the political situation. In the following months the economy took its lead from politics, rather than being "the cause" of its own instability. Tensions inside the government coalition continued to deepen. The unexpected fall of ODA chairman J. Kalvoda (for rather absurd reasons) cast a great cloud over the trustworthiness of this small political party; and another party, KDU-CSL, particularly its chairman, were behaving ostentatiously as if they did not form a part of the government coalition.

This was the moment not only for the opposition but also for Czech and foreign media and, last but not least, for influential consulting companies which had been waiting for a long time for the opportunity to "deal with" the Czech way of transformation and with our unwillingness to become a passive object of their (well-paid) advice and recommendations. But the main thing they could not forgive us for was our voucher privatization, which deprived them of a considerable part of the profits they had anticipated.

However, it has to be admitted that the government had failed to appreciate the effect that measures adopted by the CNB would have on the macro situation, on the amount of money in circulation and on aggregate demand, as well as the fact that the government dealt — more or less as a fire brigade — only with the micro effects of these steps, both on banks and companies. The government, together with the CNB and with all those extremely wise and authoritative domestic and foreign "analysts" and consultants, forecast continuing rapid growth of the economy in 1997, and this was obviously a mistake. The government based its draft of the budget on this assumption. In the end it succeeded in getting the budget passed but lacked the strength to conduct any other, more active, policy, both in view of its internal disunity and strong external pressures (from Parliament and the media).

At the beginning of 1997 the economy — with almost textbook timing — stumbled. The reason was the absence of adequate aggregate demand and that was exclusively, or at least mainly, the result of the monetary measures. The first signal came in January with the unexpected slump in budget revenues, even though this was to some extent obscured by very low temperatures and, above all, by the week-long rail strike toward the end of the month. We therefore waited impatiently for further statistics. In mid-February output data arrived confirming the slowdown, and at the beginning of March we realized that February budgetary revenues had dropped as well. It began to be evident to us in government that economic growth had come to a sudden halt.

The exchange rate was behaving in a strange way. During the politically controversial year of 1996, and at the beginning of 1997, the currency grew conspicuously stronger, despite the rise in the external imbalance caused by the asymmetrical developments of exports and imports. The crown reached its "highest" point in the middle of February 1997 when it was stronger — for instance against the German mark by 2 crowns — than a year before. This had been helped by a relatively big issue of euro crown bonds in January. Only then did a perceptible drop begin (even though it did not fall to its original par value until mid-May). It was, however, a tragic mistake that the problem was never raised between the government and the CNB. In the spring of 1997 it must have been obvious to all involved that changes in the crown's rate of exchange were totally in the hands of speculators and that it had hardly anything to do with the economy as such. The exchange rate rose despite increasingly alarming figures showing that the external imbalance continued to slide. This only confirmed the assumption that speculators were preparing to put the rate of exchange down.

The government was getting ready to intervene and was preparing radical steps in order to increase the credibility both of the government and of the economy as a whole as much as possible. However, the debate on these proposals, known as packagc No. 1, which was intended to prevent a huge budget deficit by cutting expenditures and by accelerating legislative measures intended to increase the transparency of financial markets led, as was expected, to a deep political confrontation.

Cuts in budget expenditures of 25 billion crowns (which, moreover, had to be carried out in eight months instead of 12) were, indeed, very deep. This led among other things to a further slump in aggregate demand and rather quickly slowed down investments, above all in the construction industry. As a result, the whole sector slumped. Today it can be said that the measure was probably too extreme but there were many reasons, including sending out the right signals, that we stressed the priority of a balanced budget.

The main problem with package No. 1 was that the CNB did not share our views and therefore did not deal with the problems of the currency. Only by changing the exchange rate policy, despite the surprising development of the rate, could the risk of speculative attacks on the currency be reduced. We all realized that the import deposits which we had introduced would not be seen as a credible attempt to solve the problem. Strong budgetary restrictions were therefore the only way the government could demonstrate its resolve to foreign countries while, at the same time, exerting pressure on the central bank.

Package No. 1 was a courageous political and economic step and could have played an important role in preventing both the currency crisis and the economic recession which followed. It might have achieved this goal, provided its credibility had not been undermined by Josef Lux on the very day that the government approved the plan. Perhaps some of you still remember that Lux, chairman of one of the coalition parties and a deputy prime minister with key responsibilities, declared as soon as the plan was approved that it was worthless without a thorough government reshuffle (which would in fact have meant a new government and a new coalition agreement). The positive signal which the package was intended to send out was thus almost immediately lost. This led to even more arguments, not only within the coalition government but also inside the parties themselves. In ODS for instance, vice chairman Zieleniec decided to attack me personally for allegedly suppressing a letter from the IMF. All this resulted in the destabilization both of the economy and of the political situation. A considerable role was also played by the crisis in Southeast Asia, which led to serious anxiety among investors everywhere in the world.

For a long time the CNB failed to act. It was particularly reluctant to act preventively and devalue the crown (despite the fact that the government exerted strong pressure on the bank to do it in the moment of package No. 1). The bank presumably relied on its strength, its good reputation and its considerable powers of intervention — or it had its own, completely different economic (or perhaps even political) intentions. But I do not want to speculate on this. The positive effect of all these measures was zero; the crown came under strong attack and thus an acute currency crisis began.

(c) In the chaos that followed, the CNB tried to "blow into the wind" and intervened by buying crowns to support the exchange rate. As we know, it lost roughly 3 billion dollars of its (or our) currency reserves. Simultaneously, in line with the doctrine held at the time by the IMF and accepted almost everywhere in the world, the central bank, in order to forestall the flight of foreign capital, sharply increased interest rates (the repo rate was raised from 14 to 50 per cent). This, of course, failed to prevent an onslaught by currency speculators because there was nothing to stop those who wanted to withdraw their capital. Extremely high rates of interest did not prevent the flight of capital but they did have another, perhaps intended, side-effect: the currency crisis turned into a banking crisis, then into a financial crisis and eventually into a general economic crisis which continued long after the currency crisis itself was over. The shock was too much for our fragile banking, financial and corporate sectors. One is therefore entitled to argue that the economy was not brought down by the currency crisis itself but by the way it was dealt with.

The crown was devalued by 10 percent and floated, which was certainly the right decision, albeit taken too late.

The government then decided on a second package — more as a political than an economic initiative — which meant more budget cuts (by another roughly 18 billion crowns) and tried to formulate proposals for further institutional reforms. There was also a reshuffle involving the ministers of finance and trade and industry, two prominent government members.

From a macroeconomic point of view, package No. 1 represented an unnecessary stepping up of restrictions and, as I have already said, was due more to political than economic reasons. It was an attempt to save the government and prove that it was capable of action, but it was also an attempt to demonstrate the power of those who in the autumn caused the government to fall. Politicians from all parties were trying to emancipate themselves, the media was on principle opposed to everything that was being done, and even so-called experts repeated over and over again that the first package did not go far enough and that the economy needed much stronger measures. Idolization of the IMF, which is now generally criticized for its failures and fatal mistakes precisely at the time of the 1997 currency crises, was at its peak, and any hesitation in implementing any of its recommendations was seen as arrogance, as a fundamental mistake or incompetence. Now it is, on the contrary, generally accepted that the IMF's recommendations were one of the main reasons why the crises deepened and spread.

The CNB was totally devoted to the strategy recommended by the IMF and therefore, instead of accepting that a rise in inflation in the period immediately following the crash was unavoidable, concentrated on fighting inflation even though the price that had to be paid was a devastating slump in economic performance and the risk of crisis in the entire domestic banking and corporate sphere. The CNB was, however, unwilling to discuss its policy with the government.

I cannot accept the assertion, repeated for instance by the bank's vice governor, Oldrich Dědek, that the CNB resorted to such a restrictive policy because the government was not willing to discuss institutional problems and that the CNB therefore had no choice but to save the economy, whose future stability was being jeopardized. The truth of the matter is quite the opposite. CNB representatives never showed any initiative which would have drawn attention to institutional problems, not to mention calling for a radical solution. Neither is it in the least true that the government was unwilling to debate such matters. I personally cannot imagine, given the composition of the coalition government at the time, that it would have been possible to turn down any initiative of this kind had there actually been one.

Both packages contained a number of measures aimed at moving toward a solution to some of our institutional and legal problems and imperfections. However, the political chaos that ensued prevented most of them from being implemented. They are only being implemented now, several years later. This explains why, two years after the events I am describing, most of these proposals could be incorporated into what became known as the "Dřevíč appeal" and could be presented by the media, with great clamor, as a new and fundamental initiative aimed at overcoming our problems.

The currency crises created, above all, a profound political and psychological shock. Politics and petty politics became the order of the day, and any real governance was paralyzed. The Parliament, or at least its opposition parties, turned radical, and tensions inside the governing coalition rocketed. The media, or rather politicians pretending to be journalists, launched a major counterattack.

To sum up, the currency crisis was an important reminder of the problems in our economy. It could have been avoided, and its repercussions could have been overcome, had everybody who was involved been willing to work together as partners. But that did not happen.

It is only rarely mentioned that, thanks to the relative strength of the Czech economy, the currency crisis, in the narrow sense of the word, was overcome comparatively quickly, that in the second half of 1997 the rate of exchange stabilized and gradually returned to its original value, that industrial production stabilized, and that export growth resumed. In the summer and autumn, rather surprisingly, the economy was relatively calm (despite disastrous floods). However, instead of moving forward, we suddenly found ourselves in a full-blown banking and financial crisis which turned into a general economic recession.

(d) When the worst of the currency crisis was over, the main question was whether the policies of the government and the central bank could be united in a joint effort to overcome the deep disruption caused to our banking, financial and corporate sectors.

The opposition, the smaller coalition parties, the B team inside ODS, and even the president himself, realized this was an opportunity to change the political situation, and since this was their aim, they were not too concerned about the fate of the economy. In addition, as a logical outcome of their attitudes, they interpreted the economic situation as a failure of the concept of transformation, or at least the Czech way of accomplishing it, and they therefore started a political struggle, rather than an attempt to stabilize the economy.

The shock of the currency crisis (which in itself was not as deep as is sometimes thought) was used as the main argument for discrediting the government's entire economic policy and as the tangible confirmation of its failure. It became a trigger for a political crisis. Political crisis continued in this latent form until what became known as Sarajevo, i.e., until the fall of the coalition government.

Countries such as Hungary in 1995 or South Korea in 1997 quickly managed, by using sensible policies, to regain their breath and return to growth. In our country, the central bank opted for a policy of rapidly reducing inflation to EU levels, irrespective of the impact this would have on the financially fragile business and banking sectors. In this case it was "blowing with the wind." In such circumstances it is the job of the central bank, on the contrary, to "blow into the wind."

A key factor in the development of the economy was the procedures adopted by the CNB towards the end of 1997 and during the first half of 1998. This must not be forgotten. These were primarily the introduction of inflation targets and extension of restrictive and stricter terms for the cautious running of commercial banks.

Inflation targeting is a method which is quite unsuitable for an economy in transition. After all, the announcement of an inflation target in itself had much less of an effect than our bankers assumed and, moreover, it is not a "tool" in the classic sense of the word. But what was even worse was the fact that the inflation target was set very low, and that the assessment of the transmission mechanism between monetary policy and the real economy was wrong, or rather, there was a wrong assessment of its parameters, and therefore disastrous mistakes were made in estimating actual inflation. Today it is presumably abundantly clear what we were worried about. The sudden reduction of inflation was enormously costly. And either the CNB actually aimed at such low inflation (which in a number of months in 1998 and 1999 was a deflation) or this was not what was intended, in which case low inflation was an unwanted byproduct of the CNB's policy. Targeting inflation at about 6 percent and arriving at zero resulted in a considerable spread of disinformation among companies and to an unnecessarily high nominal movement of salaries and wages and of some other budgetary expenditures.

More important than creating expectations by setting targets for inflation were monetary macro restrictions, chief among them being the late reductions in nominal interest rates, or to put it differently, the fact that they were falling more slowly than inflation. This resulted in a disastrous rise in real interest rates, even though this was quite unnecessary. It is perhaps too obvious to have to explain that what the economy needed at this point was movement in exactly the opposite direction and that there was no reason why the banks and companies should have been further restricted. But these measures were not adopted by accident. The extreme independence of our central bank meant that it followed solely its own interests. And I do not even want to speculate whether this was just bad economics, or a well thought-out policy.

When I talked about more stringent conditions for commercial banks, I had in mind:

- the requirement by the CNB for additional reserves to cover mortgages on unpaid loans and
- higher requirements concerning the consolidated balances of commercial banks.

Statistics indicate that these measures, introduced at such a time, further increased the costs incurred by our banks, that their hitherto profitable results turned into losses and that to all intents and purposes this prevented them from granting any more loans. This was the last blow to our economy which then, with a boomerang effect, returned from companies back to the banks. It is not a question of whether these measures were or were not in themselves economically rational and, from a banking point of view, sufficiently circumspect. The only question must be whether they were carried out at the right time.

All in all, I would suggest that, given the considerable passivity, and at the same time almost irrelevance, of government fiscal policy (due to the floating exchange rate), the monetary policy did not help to stabilize the economy and led to exactly the opposite, to widespread economic recession. There is no easy way out of recession, as we can see even now, but that is a different topic altogether.

II. General conclusions

Unfortunately the Czech economy in the second half of the '90s had all four of these characteristics:

- a fixed rate of exchange;
- immature (fragile, vulnerable) banking and financial institutions;
- an economy which is totally open to a strongly interlinked (or in today's parlance "globalized") world; and
- any macroeconomic disturbance (inflation, current account deficit, budget deficit).

Which of them could have been avoided?

- There was no need for a fixed rate of exchange, but I do not believe that this would have fundamentally altered the situation. Speculative capital would have probably moved around in the same way. The movements would have probably created an unwelcome exchange bubble, first moving up and then rapidly sinking. The central bank would "only" not have had to squander billions of dollars on an intervention which was condemned to failure, but it can be assumed that it would have intervened against a sharp drop in the exchange rate anyway and would not have permitted clean floating.
- It was not possible for the banking and financial institutions to be better and less unstable than they were. The idea that more regulation and supervision from above would improve their quality is wrong. All these institutions were passing through a stage in their development that could not be avoided.
- Perhaps we could have been less open to the outside world because, in this respect in particular, there was no need to be ahead of other countries in a similar position.
- It is unlikely that the macroeconomic situation could have been completely different. The central bank did not have to have such ambitious inflation targets.

And so, in my view, much more important than these economic "fundamentals" was the failure of "crisis management," i.e., of the reaction to crisis. All economically positive periods in history have been judged not by their achievements but by the way they ended. And that is also the problem of our era. The previous period was positive but its end negated everything.

By the same token, it is now clear that structural reforms, which were announced or carried out at the time of crisis did not have, and could not have had, any short-term effect. They could only send a signal that our country was trying to cope with the situation.

It was shown, once again, that the most important aspect is correct timing. Macroeconomic policy should have been moderately restrictive before, certainly not after, the event.

There is a vast literature on currency crises, but the key dilemma remains unresolved. The writers have not answered the question of whether currency crises were — given the conditions prevailing at the time — avoidable or not.

There are, of course, a number of elegant textbook solutions, but transition economies do not lend themselves to textbook solutions. It is therefore my view that this kind of crisis could not have been wholly avoided. But they could have run a completely different course and had different consequences.

Remarks on the Occasion of Awarding Milton Friedman an Honorary Doctoral Degree

Prague School of Economics, April 17, 1997

It is for me a great pleasure and, at the same time, a great honor to participate in this ceremony and to have the opportunity to say a few words about Milton Friedman and his role in economic science and economic policy in the second half of the 20th century. There is no doubt that Milton Friedman, Nobel Prize winner and a laureate of many other prestigious international prizes and awards, is one of the most distinguished economists of this century. His ideas influenced whole generations of economists, not only in his own country, the United States, and in the Western world, but in our part of the world as well. In the communist era, people like me did not have the slightest chance to dream about meeting him, but I can confess that there were many spiritual links between Friedman and some of us even at that time. I myself spent years studying his works as well as the works of his colleagues at the University of Chicago.

It is a paradox that in spite of our relative isolation from the rest of the world at that time, I have been in the past often called a Friedmanite, a monetarist or an exponent of the Chicago School. I always took it as an honor; however, those who used such labels meant it as an offense or an accusation.

Reading and studying Friedman's works helped me and many of us to understand economic reality, to understand economics, to understand its methodology, the role of the market in society, the role of the state in a free market economy, the role of money in the economy, etc. Surely there were other influential authors but there was no one comparable in intellectual and human integrity, in firmness of professional and ideological stances and attitudes, in innovative boldness, in simplicity and clarity of exposition and in the scope and quality of important contributions both to economic theory and to the theory of public policy. At the same time I do not know anyone else with such personal charm, as well as the ability to pay attention to other people and their words and ideas. Meeting him for the first time in 1990 was a real enjoyment and an unforgettable experience.

In the theoretical field I consider as absolutely crucial his 1956 *Restatement of the Quantity Theory of Money* and the subsequent literature in this field, his theory of the demand for money, his program for monetary stability, his theory of nominal income, his inflation-unemployment tradeoff, to name just a few of his articles, all of which represent the most important contributions to the theory of money and monetary policy.

His *Essays in Positive Economics* was methodologically no less important. Friedman's clear and persuasive explanation of the differences between positive and normative economics, as well as his arguments about instrumentalism of scientific assumptions, influenced the way many of us look at economic theory and economic reality. I must say that it is also important methodological advice for everyday life in public policy. In very recent days, when discussing both in the government and in public the consequences of recent shifts in monetary policy in this country, I used several times his stress on the importance of time lags, of the so-called recognition, decision-making and implementation lags in economic policy.

Friedman's persuasive arguments about economic policy, about fixed vs. flexible rules, about monetarism vs. Keynesianism were discussed for many decades in Western countries, but I know that he knows that we discussed them in the former communist Czechoslovakia as well. I have to confess that the same disputes stay with us today. Yesterday afternoon I announced the Czech government's decision to change the macroeconomic policy as a reaction to the slowing down of economic growth and, as a consequence, to the slowing down of state budget revenues. If my analysis is correct — and in this respect, I am a good pupil of Milton Friedman because I believe that "money matters" — the problem we face now is connected with last summer's change in monetary policy. I wish our bankers would have followed the fixed rules proposition of Milton Friedman at that time.

Friedman is, however, not only a theoretician in the very rigorous discipline of economic science. He is at the same time a true believer in the unrestricted market economy and I believe that his books *Capitalism and Freedom*, together with the more recent *Free to Choose,* opened the eyes of whole generations, not only of scholars, but also of ordinary citizens on all the continents of this planet.

All that helped us to understand the tenets of the old communist regime and its oppressive character and economic irrationality. With Friedman as our background, we had no dreams about the so-called Third Ways, about perestroika, about the reformability of communism. Friedman helped us interpret the actual communist economy not as a textbook command economy, based on directives going in the vertical direction from the central planning commission at the top to individual firms, but as a very strange and truncated market economy with imperfect, but nevertheless dominant horizontal relations among economic agents at the micro level. Friedman knew that it was impossible to suppress human behavior, the spontaneity of exchange, implicit if not explicit prices, widespread bargaining, etc. It was a very rare attitude at that time.

At the same time, the works of Milton Friedman helped us understand the logic of the transformation of a communist country into a free society and a full-fledged market economy. Because of him, we had a clear vision where to go and a pragmatic strategy for how to get there. We did not want to mastermind the whole process because it would not be possible and definitely not successful. We knew we had to trust free citizens to create the new world with only moderate help from above.

I am sure the Prague School of Economics will be honored to have such an honorary doctor and I believe that to have Milton Friedman as our graduate will be a strong positive motivation for all future students and collaborators of this school.

The Preaching of George Stigler and His Impact upon the End of Communism and the Formation of a Free Society

George Stigler Memorial Lecture, University of Chicago, May 4, 1998

It is a great and extraordinary honor for me to be invited to deliver this Memorial Lecture. It is a great honor because of George Stigler himself, because of the preeminence of the two previous speakers (George Shultz and Milton Friedman) and, finally, because of the enormous prestige of the University of Chicago.

I am probably the only one in this room who did not know Stigler personally, who met him only very briefly at the Mont Pelerin Society Meeting in Munich (in September 1990) where he attended my speech about the collapse of communism in Central and Eastern Europe.[14] However, I had been reading his works for decades during the communist era, starting with his textbook, *The Theory of Price*, which was quite accidentally (and, of course, illegally) translated into Czech at the Institute of Economics of the Czechoslovak Academy of Sciences prior to the Soviet occupation in 1968.[15]

There is no doubt that Stigler belonged among the most influential, most productive, most innovative and most consistent economists in the second half of this century, that he influenced several generations of American (as well as foreign) economists, that he made an enormous contribution to the Chicago school of economics and that he stood firmly on the side of those who believed more in markets than in the capability of governments. This is well known and I do not possess any comparative advantage in assessing his work and intellectual heritage, especially to this audience.

I will, therefore, try to use my special perspective, which may perhaps reveal something different, because it comes from the outside, from someone who spent most of his life in a world which was based on totally different ideas and policies. I must admit, however, that this is not my first speech devoted to George Stigler. In the communist era, between 1979 and 1985, I succeeded in using (or perhaps misusing) a relatively minor and therefore irrelevant institution, the Czechoslovak Society for the Promotion of Science and Technology, to organize a regular economic seminar, which at that time became the meeting place for many nonconformist economists and social scientists. Afterward, this group was the main supplier of members for the first post-communist government in my country, which was formed at the end of 1989. Once a year the topic of the seminar was the Nobel Prize in Economics, and a lecture, given mostly by me, was used to present non-Marxist economic theory and market-oriented ideas. The lectures were published in an internal bulletin (in several hundred copies) and in a book in 1991.[16]

I intend to use my arguments from 1982 now, mainly for two reasons:

- to demonstrate what was known in Prague at that time (when so-called bourgeois or non-Marxist economics was considered wrong, dangerous and useless); and
- to show what we (or I) then considered as most relevant for our intellectual enrichment.

I hope this approach will be productive.

1. Sixteen years ago, I started stressing and admiring Stigler´s conservatism, his individualism, his criticism of government interventionism — all of which was very rare, especially in the '50s and '60s. I quoted mostly from his famous 1964 Presidential Address to the American Economic Association, "The Economist and the State."[17] His very strong message — similar to that of Milton Friedman, Mises and Hayek — was extremely important for us. I mentioned as well his warning that our philosophy or ideology should not dominate or substitute for economic analysis and that our economic policy suggestions should not express our personal tastes or preferences but should be based on a serious theoretical and empirical work. Looking at the economic literature and policy recommendations, I am afraid that the economists do not pay enough attention to these aspects of Stigler's work.

Stigler believed neither in the motivation of the state to intervene in the economy (which was afterward developed in the Public Choice School writings), nor in the capability of the state to intervene rationally (which is more a Hayekian argument). Both points are absolutely crucial. I also remember that I stressed his warning about the dangers of amateur politicization by economists. He suggested on the contrary to always compare costs and benefits of alternative institutional settings and economic policy solutions. It is probably not necessary to stress here that our communist experience demonstrated to us very clearly that the costs of irrational institutional arrangements could be enormous.

2. The centrally administered economy was — at least at first sight — dominated by vertical relations (it was, therefore, described as a command economy),

not by horizontal ones. That is probably the main reason why we originally studied (and understood) more macroeconomics than microeconomic theory. However, Stigler never paid any attention to the macroeconomic field. For him economic theory was identical with the price theory. He used price theory as his main instrument of analysis; he tried to apply it in many nontraditional fields of inquiry. For instance, in his article with Gary Becker "De Gustibus non Est Disputandum,"[18] he stressed that we should not look too much beyond the two crucial variables, prices and incomes, for the explanation of human behavior, and that we should not passively wait for the explanation of various economic phenomena from other behavioral sciences. This "pure economism" helped us look at the communist command economy in a new way, and to come up with some surprising observations about its distorted economic character, which should be analyzed with economic *instrumentarium*, or intellectual tools, not with psychology or political science.

3. Stigler, together with Milton Friedman, believed in the instrumentalism of economic assumptions (see his 1947 polemics about marginalism),[19] in the productivity of a proper hypothesis, in the comparative advantage of its predictive power regardless of its realism. It was extremely important for the defense of abstract theories, of theories which we learned at that time from textbooks without having teachers and instructors. Without theories, one lives in a world of empiricism and of historicism, in a world of attempts to "describe" reality, which is, of course, a hopeless endeavor.

Stigler's approach was connected with his strong emphasis on quantitative economic analysis — especially in the fields of market structure, price flexibility (or rigidity), duopoly or oligopoly structure and behavior, antitrust legislation, etc. Many of us were at that time victims of playing with sophisticated macroeconometric models and, as a result, elementary empirical analysis was almost nonexistent.

4. I was aware of the fact that Stigler received the Nobel Prize for his work on regulation. In his 1971 article, he argued that regulation frequently reduced competition, that regulation was done mostly on behalf of regulated firms and not of consumers and that it often made matters worse rather than better. Because our libraries had only several Western economic journals and the *Bell Journal of Economics* was not among them, I did not read his famous article at the moment of writing my speech and I knew it from quotations only. But Stigler's

ideas coincided fully with our experience. Even though the whole immodest "communist" planning (not just modest "capitalist" regulation) was done "from below," the actual planning power was in the hands of the "planned" firms, not in the hands of the Central Planning Commission.

5. Finally, I would like to mention another field — the economics of information and Stigler's 1961 seminal article.[20] The idea that any information is a good like any other, that it has its costs and that there is, therefore, a supply of and a demand for it was a simple but crucial contribution. In the countries of Central and Eastern Europe, we constantly discussed the search for an optimum degree of centralization and decentralization of economic decision-making and we used Stigler's approach as another way of attacking the nature of the command economy.

I just mentioned five basic points I stressed in my speech in 1982 and I have to repeat that all of them helped us to understand and later dismantle the old, inefficient and oppressive regime. *Because ideas have consequences.*

What to add to it in 1998? There is no doubt that eight years after the collapse of communism, the market economy in my country and elsewhere works. It is not perfect, and especially the markets are not perfect, but from the economic theory point of view we know — together with George Stigler — that the best way to prevent monopolistic practices is to encourage domestic and especially foreign competition. Therefore, we liberalized markets without waiting for a perfect market structure. We accepted Stigler's concept of a minimalist antitrust policy and of a minimalist market regulation. With the benefit of hindsight we may argue, however, that more regulation in capital markets could have prevented some recent problems of our economy, but I am afraid of the misuse of government intervention and have trouble accepting it *a priori*. It is difficult to constructively generate markets. It is very easy to kill them or to block their spontaneous evolution. And I hope that this is exactly what Stigler would say if he were here with us today.

There is no doubt as well that a change in institutional arrangements has its costs, that there is not only no free lunch but also no free reform. We paid quite heavily in lost output and income and this was — and is — difficult to explain to the citizens of a country undergoing transformation who expect a visible and tangible betterment of their living conditions.

In *the first stage*, the reforms "worked." After a short and inevitable economic decline which lasted two or three years and represented the healthy shakeoff of nonviable economic activities associated with the old economic system, the economy began to recover. The growth rate of GDP reached the 4 to 6 percent range in following years (three consecutive years in our case), the investment ratio became extremely high, domestic spending visibly grew, imports skyrocketed and foreign capital inflows as a share of GDP were enormous.

I believed in the possibility of a longer continuation of such a relatively smooth development. The experience of the last two years — let's call this *the second stage* — tells us, however, that we have underestimated the enormous vulnerability of such an economy (even if I think that it was, probably, more our inability to change it than our underestimation of this vulnerability). The economy became characterized by:

- dangerously growing expectations of all economic agents (consumers as well as investors) and our inability to slow them down without heavy political costs;
- overinvestment (from the macroeconomic point of view) both in directly productive and nondirectly productive activities, which led to investment-saving disequilibrium;
- a growing trade imbalance which was gradually accompanied by balance of payments´ current account deficits;
- slow improvements in the institutional framework, weak regulation of monopolistic or otherwise nonperfect markets and unsystematic law enforcement;
- the disturbances connected with aggressive and merciless global capital markets, especially when they were confronted with weak domestic banking and financial intermediation.

As a result, the second stage led to an economic slowdown (or stagnation) and to a political crisis, which meant the interruption of the previous, relatively smooth development. Markets became nervous about both the trade deficit and the strong currency. As a result of it, capital inflows stopped, interest rates rose, the economy slowed down, tax revenues declined, fiscal balance deteriorated, state budget expenditures had to be dramatically cut, the economy slowed down even more, capital was pulled out of the country, the currency depreciated, some firms and banks got into troubles, the economy went into a very sluggish growth, etc. The anatomy of crisis was rather simple (and well-known).

I am sure George Stigler's name will stay with us and we will learn a lot by rereading (and new generations of economists by reading) his works. He was realistically skeptical about the science of economics (but called it, proudly, the imperialistic science among social sciences) but I like very much his witty saying that "the economic theory of economists is much better than the economic theory of anyone else's," which is not an empty joke. We — and especially we in the first decade of a market economy — live in a world where everyone has strong opinions about economic issues but not everyone has looked into George Stigler's and similar works. I am sure that without Stigler, the economic theory of economists would have been less developed than it is now. I hope we are all aware of it. If not, this is what I wanted to say in my 1998 George Stigler Memorial Lecture.

The Importance of the Public Choice School both for the Criticism of the Centrally Planned Economy and for the Process of Dismantling It

European Society of Public Choice Conference, Prague, January, 1998

The process of critically assessing the centrally planned economy, which in my own case began around the mid-1960s, evolved in the former communist countries through several stages. These stages of development in our thinking reflected to a considerable extent our relative isolation from the course of the worldwide economic discussion of the matter. Nevertheless, they partly reflected the major tendencies and schools of economic thinking.

The first stage was a nontheoretical and nonconceptual critique stemming from the feelings of individuals living in a malfunctioning economic system, individuals who daily observed its irrationalities and who soon came to the understanding that the system was basically wrong. This critique was already based on the more or less subconscious understanding of the impossibility and therefore redundancy of attempts to centrally administer the whole economy in which nobody can (or is able to) influence significantly millions of daily occurring decisions at a distance and from an administrative center. At the same time we felt that without the existence of private property and a chance to win or lose everything, the economic agents lack adequate incentives for rational behavior.

During this period the first attempts to partially improve this flawed system began to take place everywhere around us. They proceeded along two main routes, both of which reacted to the discussion in economic theory.

The first stream of thinking was represented by proposals to improve central planning (evolving from the ideas of Barone and his branch of the Lausanne School all the way to the mathematical illusions of the Soviet optimal planners, such as Kantorovich, Nemchinov and Novozhilov, or to the cybernetic and system engineering dreams of Forrester, the Club of Rome and their East European followers). These proposals were not based on the market; all of them were based on belief in the feasibility of "managing" the economy from the center. I have never shared this belief, not even at the turn of the 1950s and 1960s as a student of the Prague School of Economics without the slightest chance to put my hands on the work of a Western economist, having to study Marxist political economy and using only my common sense. Even today I am still convinced that powerful computers do not represent the solution to the information problem of the centrally planned economy. I also do not believe in the so-called information revolution. My persistent doubts have been only enriched with additional arguments after reading Stigler's "Economics of Information," which I discovered with a 20-year delay.[21]

The other route of reform attempts was represented by partial concessions to the market, by various combinations of plan and market, and by the acceptance of the market as a tool of central planning. As a fresh university graduate and a post-graduate student at the Economic Institute of the Czechoslovak Academy of Sciences in Prague, I was confronted with this approach at the second half of the 1960s. This approach culminated during the so-called Prague Spring. It was an *a priori* lost battle to improve the centrally planned economy without a fundamental change of the system itself. In those days, it was an illusion that infected not only Czechoslovakia and the communist world, but to a large extent also the Western world. We may recall the then-very popular convergence theory (see the well-known work of Tinbergen) which unfortunately echoes even today.[22] Nonetheless, it does so in the West more than in the East. Compared to the West, the East has been cured much better by its own experience.

In Czechoslovakia, a relatively narrow group of my peers discovered modern economic theory and its standard defense of the market economy at that time. At the same moment — and with a half-century delay — we rediscovered the famous "controversy about socialism," which took place in economics in the 1920s and 1930s.[23] At least for me, the argumentation there was fundamental. I then translated and published the excerpts of the major ideas of Mises and Hayek representing one side of the controversy, and Lange and Lerner representing the opposite side. Already then I found the arguments of the key representatives of the Austrian school absolutely convincing. I accepted the ideas concerning the impossibility of establishing a properly functioning market under socialism, i.e., without the existence of private property (so succinctly stated in the famous work of Mises from 1920).[24] Correspondingly, the Austrian School emphasized the fact that information is time- and space-dependent, dispersed at the micro level and tied with the specific economic activities and that a transmission of information to any economic center is impossible, not because of an imperfect communication technology but because of the inner substance of this information. These arguments were instrumental for my criticism of the reform concepts formulated by Ota Šik and his colleagues (these thoughts were canonically formulated in a number of Hayek's works, above all in his well-known paper "The Use of Knowledge in Society"[25]). Already then we put forward these arguments loudly. We were often scolded since we were undermining the authority of the very popular reformers. However, these reforms soon ceased being topical. Any potential evolution of these reforms toward something different and more substantial was abruptly stopped — at least for us — in August 1968 after the invasion of the Warsaw Pact armies into Czechoslovakia. And for me personally, one phase of my life came to an end: I had to terminate my career as a theoretician and research fellow.

During the following years we were at least trying to read the standard economic literature. The common and therefore not overly deep, revealing and not at all theoretical Western sovietologic literature did not give us many new ideas. Nevertheless, it contributed to our understanding that the socialist economy was administered rather than planned (after the well-known paper of Gregory Grossman from the 1960s and the extremely valuable work of Walter Eucken on the economy of fascist Germany, which had been published after the war) and that it was the economy of a conflict of interests rather than the economy of perfect or "so far" imperfect planning.[26] We began to view this economy as the one where the dominant relationships were not vertical but horizontal ones (the idea about the dominance of the vertical linkages was and still is a cornerstone of the economic and sociologic theories of socialism), no matter how strange and distorted these relationships were, given the absence of well-defined property rights and the existence of disequilibrium and therefore wrong prices.

This way of thinking was developed by an interesting branch of the Czech school of economic thought in the 1970s. This group, which was represented most visibly by Luboš Mlčoch, more or less departed from the standard economic *instrumentarium* and applied game theory to the analysis of the centrally planned economy. Using this approach, it distinguished a cooperative "game of planning" from a very noncooperative "game about the plan," which means to achieve the best plan for oneself. It talked about the steering pyramid upside down, reminded us that a planning process goes from below rather than from above, in parallel with the expression "economic power" introduced the expression "planning power," and emphasized that planning power was not entirely concentrated in the economic center.

The complete isolation of the Czech economists and absence of any chance to publish these ideas openly in Czechoslovakia, not to mention publishing them abroad, led us not to formulate our ideas in a comprehensive way and they remained largely "ideas." Nevertheless, I can say that we were quite well prepared when we first discovered the works of the Public Choice School which reached Czechoslovakia. They came with a significant delay, brought about (besides other factors) by the difficulties which the Public Choice School faced when it encountered mainstream economic theory and the dominant conflict between monetarism and Keynesian theory at that time. I have to admit that even the two or three libraries where some major economic journals were available during the '70s gave me no chance to come across the most significant works of the Public Choice School, especially those of Buchanan or Tullock.[27]

Since the end of the 1970s, despite constant resistance from the communist regime, I had been regularly organizing a seminar on economic theory and economic policy (these series were irrevocably terminated as late as 1986), celebrating annually the latest Nobel Prize winners. The seminars gave me a good chance to review the main ideas of the winners and to give a public lecture explaining their contribution. It was only in 1986, when the Nobel Prize was awarded to James Buchanan, that I fully appreciated his work. I began to understand the gradual but logical development of his thinking from the discussion of the problems of "finance" to "public finance" and finally to "public choice theory." Buchanan, more than anyone else, clearly understood that it was impossible to tackle the public finance problem without clarifying first what the adjective "public" really meant. He and his colleagues focused on the process of public or collective choice, as opposed to the standard economic analysis of private choice. Buchanan's assumption that in fact there is no such thing as collective or public choice, that every decision is always a private matter, proved to be a revolution, although now it appears to be rather obvious. It was a radical breakthrough in the analysis of behavior of government in a capitalist system. We immediately grasped the idea because it was even more important for the analysis of a socialist system where the role of the government was much more prominent than even in the most interventionist-minded capitalist countries.

From our own experience we intuitively understood that the "public interest" does not exist as such, that there is nobody who represents it. We understood that there is nothing like a social welfare function, which became the object of a famous discussion between Buchanan and Arrow. (It does not mean, however, that there is no such thing as a public good.) We clearly saw the partiality of all interests pushed through by different pressure groups and we always saw a concrete individual hidden behind the "public interest."

The public choice arguments were important, even if we had discarded the centrally planned economy concept without it. Most economists, sociologists and political scientists at that time, though, studied socialist systems with a top-bottom perspective, as if it were a society managed completely by the state's and party's bureaucracy. This concept was clearly unsatisfactory, and public choice theory helped to make this evident. Public choice theory was equally important for our search of the rational (meaning the least burdensome) way of transforming socialist society. In our understanding, "government was not a romanticized generator of public goods or a protector of virtue," and this gave new arguments to our critique of the centrally planned (or administered) economy.

The Public Choice School demystified the political decision-making process. This was also true (and perhaps even more so) for a socialist society with no political democracy. The absence of democracy further amplified the consequences of "government failure," which was another important term coined by the Public Choice School. The critique of welfare economics by Buchanan and other representatives of the Public Choice School, who lucidly explained that although welfare economics analyzed the market failure concept, it lacked the understanding that "market failure simply means the failure of real world markets to achieve the standards of the imaginary market" and said absolutely nothing about the degree of government failure, was well received.[28] We also welcomed the criticism of government regulation, the criticism that "regulation" is "a way for sellers already in the market to use government coercion to restrict competition, choice and opportunities."[29]

To summarize, public choice theory significantly enriched our critique of the centrally planned economy with further important aspects. It gave us completely new tools for the analysis of this economy and prepared us for its final dismantling.

Economists of the Austrian School — namely Mises and Hayek — and Chicago economists — especially Friedman, Stigler and Becker — provided us with a blueprint of the system we wanted to establish. Therefore, when the chance came in 1989, we did not look for any "third ways." (I said in January 1990 in Davos that "the third way is the fastest way to the third world.") The Public Choice School prepared us for a fight with the proponents of various third ways, of interventionism, of a welfare state, of a social-oriented market economy. We did not trust the state (even moreso than has become standard in the West these days), but new arguments for our distrust stemmed from our practical experience rather than from theory. As we became ministers of finance or prime ministers almost overnight, we had to "play" the state. I am aware of the crucial role of the government in the moment of transformation, and I know what should remain in the state domain afterward, but at the same time I know that the government can never make efficient and competent microeconomic decisions. Unfortunately, we have been forced to make many such decisions during the last few years, but we always felt that they were rather "leaps to the darkness" as Mises described it (because neither the prime minister nor the minister of finance ever invests his own money). We could not make such decisions well, no matter how hard we tried.

We knew, therefore, that we needed the fastest and broadest privatization of the whole economy and we never listened to the advice of experts from international financial institutions who spent a long time in disputes on whether the restructuring of the firms should precede or follow privatization. We also knew that a quick and full opening of domestic markets and liberalization of prices and foreign trade were needed, and we strived to limit significantly the scale of microeconomic intervention. As a result, we had to live with imperfect markets, but we knew that the functioning of the state is even less perfect. It can be documented in many ways. The dismantling of the State Planning Commission, legalization of private entrepreneurship and radical deregulation and liberalization did not lead to a perfect market. These steps, though, contributed to the fundamental destruction of the previous behavioral stereotypes and of the spontaneously created "rules of the game." It was the privatization that irrefutably signaled that transformation is a serious thing. Unfortunately, the advocates (mainly foreign) of gradual approaches to privatization and deregulation have never understood this.

The Public Choice School clearly defines the border between the private and the public. This sharp border serves as a very important defense line against the rent-seeking behavior of enterprises and their demands for "the soft financing" or "the soft budget constraint." All our enterprises were well versed in these demands from the old socialist days. During socialism we were, of course, a "society of interest groups" and only those who understood the contribution of the Public Choice School know why it is so crucial to have such an unmistakable border between the private and the public. The supporters of popular but empty concepts such as "a friendly society," "a civil society" or "an ecosocial market economy" have not understood this contribution and it is the reason for their proposals to make this border fuzzy. This approach opens the way for political rent-seeking, for influence upon political decisions and for redistribution of state finances aimed at satisfying the partial interests of organized interest groups of producers and other various lobbying groups (professional associations, trade unions, associations of tenants or of landlords, etc.). The aim of these groups is to strip the state of its powers, of course in their own interest, and that is why — often under a banner of misinterpreted decentralization projects — they call for the delegation of state power down to the lower levels (but in fact toward these groups representing partial interests). These are attempts to create a partialized and weak state and to gradually transform free society into a corporativist one.

Our "velvet" revolution has broken our past habits and for the first period afterwards created a certain vacuum because it radically weakened the redistributive pressure groups. I would like to recall in this respect the ideas of M. Olson published in 1982 in his *The Rise and Decline of Nations.*[30] In this book I was confronted with the notion of the rent-seeking society for the first time. M. Olson also carefully distinguished the countries that have been stable (and therefore more and more rigid) for a long time and those in which radical social movements broke rent-seeking activities for a while. The immediate consequence of our revolution was the existence of this vacuum of power and we tried to use the situation to put through fast and radical transformation of the system. We did not give the interest groups any opportunity to consolidate and strengthen their positions in the economy and the entire society.

This leads me to thoughts on the reform strategy. Interventionists kept contemplating the optimal sequencing of reform measures for years and years, whereas in the meantime we were discussing the speed of it, due to the concern about both the political opposition (which was also weak in the very beginning) and the economic "opposition" represented in the market economy by the phenomenon of rent-seeking. The obvious conclusion following from the theory of rent-seeking was that it is much easier to achieve a fundamental reform when moving fast and not gradually, in partial steps. If such a favorable post-revolutionary situation had been missed, the transformation would have melted down into attempts at partial and small modifications easily wrecked by the economic opposition of those interest groups. The opponents of the fast and radical reform strategy do not comprehend this, which demonstrates that they have either never read or have not carefully read the literature about public choice. The opponents of our transformation strategy often do not understand that politics is neither a formulation of theoretical blueprints, nor their implementation by an enlightened powerful elite. Instead, politics is a process of bargaining and fighting with existing pressure groups.

Those countries that did not seize the favorable moment wasted the historical chance which might perhaps never be repeated. The political enthusiasm for fundamental changes inevitably fades in time and parallel to that is a consolidation of various interest groups.

Confidence in the market is completely in line with the public choice approach. James Buchanan clearly says: "Public choice does not say that the market is perfect. That is not part of it. But it says that politics fail."[31] In his 1994 lecture "Politicized Economies in Limbo," he recalls that systemic reforms are very complex, and I would add that they are not free either.[32] Except for the initial interest of citizens in the political change of the regime, there is no aggregative interest in the promised increase in the aggregate value of output. Buchanan stressed that "almost all commentators proceed as if such an aggregative interest exists," although there is no country in the world in which one can (or could ever) find a "direct, action-motivated interest in economic prosperity," since only "particular distributional interests" exist.[33]

These interests are exactly the key ones, at least for me. Robert J. Barro recalled the empirical regularity that "more democracy typically enhances the power of interest groups."[34] This is the correct description of the process we are experiencing at present in our country. A rebirth of democracy is intertwined with an extraordinary fear of the authoritarian state and this weakens democracy in its battle with various pressure groups. This battle represents the next stage of the transformation process and our triumph or failure in it will determine the further development of our society.

The Public Choice School has armed us with the weapons needed to fight this battle successfully.

Footnotes to Chapter II

[1] Remarks by Ricardo Hausmann.

[2] Joseph Stiglitz, "Financial Systems for Eastern Europe's Emerging Democracies," International Center for Economic Growth, San Francisco, Occasional Paper, No. 38, 1993.

[3] Ibid., p. 7.

[4] Ibid., p. 32

[5] Ibid., p. 15.

[6] Václav Klaus, 1997 Annual Hayek Memorial Lecture, "The Transformation of the Czech Society: Retrospect and Prospect," Institute of Economic Affairs, London, June 17, 1997.

[7] Václav Klaus, *The Rebirth of Liberty in the Heart of Europe* (Washington, D.C.: Cato Institute, 1997).

[8] More arguments can be found in my book *Renaissance: The Rebirth of Liberty in the Heart of Europe* (Washington, D.C.: Cato Institute, 1997), especially chapter 10, and in my "A Short or Long Way to Privatization," in *An Austrian in France, Festschrift in Honor of Jacques Garello* (Torino: La Rosa Editrice, 1997).

[9] "Policy Dilemmas of Eastern European Reforms: Notes of an Insider," in "Central Banking Issues in Emerging Market-Oriented Economies," symposium sponsored by the Federal Reserve Bank of Kansas City, Jackson Hole, Wyoming, August 23-25, 1990.

[10] See my "Creating a Stable Monetary Order," in *Renaissance: The Rebirth of Liberty in the Heart of Europe* (Washington, D.C.: Cato Institute, 1997).

[11] Similar arguments were raised by the president of the Federal Reserve Bank of Kansas City, Thomas M. Hoenig, in his recent speech, published in the *Federal Reserve Bank of Kansas City Economic Review*, March 1997.

[12] Joseph Stiglitz, "Financial Systems for Eastern Europe's Emerging Democracies," International Center for Economic Growth, San Francisco, Occasional Paper No. 38, 1993, p. 32.

[13] Ibid., p. 15.

[14] Václav Klaus, "Main Obstacles to Rapid Economic Transformation of Eastern Europe," in "A Road to Market Economy," TOP Agency, Prague 1991.

[15] George J. Stigler, *The Theory of Price* (New York: Macmillan, 1946).

[16] Václav Klaus, *Ekonomická věda a ekonomická reforma* (Prague: GENNEX, 1991).

[17] George Stigler, "The Economist and the State," *American Economic Review*, No. 1, March 1965.

[18] George Stigler and Gary Becker, "De Gustibus non Est Disputandum," *American Economic Review*, No. 1, March 1977.

[19] George Stigler, "Professor Lester and the Marginalists," *American Economic Review*, No. 1, March 1947.

[20] George Stigler, "The Economics of Information," *Journal of Political Economy*, No. 3, June 1961.

[21] Ibid.

[22] Jan Tinbergen, "Do Communist and Free Economies Show Converging Pattern?" *Soviet Studies*, April 1961.

[23] A. Bergson, "Socialist Economics," in *A Survey of Contemporary Economics* (Homewood, Illinois, 1948).

[24] Ludwig von Mises, "Die Wirtschaftsrechnung im sozialistischen Gemeinwesen," *Archiv für Sozialwissenschaften*, April 1920.

[25] F. A. Hayek, "The Use of Knowledge in Society," *American Economic Review*, September 1945.

[26] Gregory Grossman, "Notes for a Theory of the Command Economy," *Soviet Studies*, October, 1963; and Walter Eucken, "On the Theory of the Centrally Administered Economy: An Analysis of the German Experiment," *Economica*, 1948.

[27] Including James Buchanan and Gordon Tullock, *The Calculus of Consent* (Ann Arbor: University of Michigan Press, 1962).

[28] W. C. Mitchell and R. T. Simons, *Beyond Politics: Markets, Welfare, and the Failure of Bureaucracy* (Boulder, Co.: Westview Press, 1994), p. 6.

[29] Ibid.

[30] Mancur Olson, *The Rise and Decline of Nations* (New Haven, Conn.: Yale University Press, 1982).

[31] Interview for *The Region*, Federal Reserve Bank of Minneapolis, No. 3, 1995.

[32] James Buchanan, "Politicized Economies in Limbo," lecture notes, 1994.

[33] James Buchanan, "The Economic Theory of Politics Reborn," *Challenge*, March-April 1988.

[34] Robert J. Barro, "Determinants of Democracy," Mont Pelerin Society General Meeting, Vienna, September 1996.

Václav Klaus and his wife, Livia Klausova, Telč, Czech Republic, May 2004.

Chapter III:

EUROPE AND ITS INTEGRATION

European Monetary Union and Its Systemic and Fiscal Consequences

Notes for New Atlantic Initiative Luncheon, Washington, D.C., September 30, 1996

The European Monetary Union as a distinct political, and therefore not purely economic, project has at present become one of the dominant political goals of the European integration process and will undoubtedly remain in this position for a long time. It is more a political goal of politicians than a goal of European citizens, but because we live in the era of indirect, representative democracy, the difference is not so important from the view of decision-making processes. In any case we can say that the decision to create the European Monetary Union is the most important one taken since the end of World War II. Despite this fact, I cannot resist the impression that the problems regarding the European Monetary Union — because of the fact that it is predominantly a political endeavor — are being trivialized, that we overestimate its — however indisputable — advantages, and, on the contrary, that we ignore or fully omit its disadvantages.

It is quite clear that the main advantage — but I wish to mention that it is only for the ones who are moving, not the ones who do not move or do not move enough — is the possibility to move within one monetary area, without having to exchange money every hundred kilometers, without being victims of unexpected devaluations or revaluations and so on. But nothing is free and our main task is to find out whether the benefits of monetary integration will prevail over the costs and whether its costs and benefits will coincide in time.

These are not minor considerations. These are not the concerns of a "Europessimist." These are the concerns voiced by a responsible politician, and, I would add, a politician who has spent the majority of his life in a communist regime, where the basic structural characteristics were not central planning, not state ownership, not even the dominant role of the Communist Party, but the priority of politics over economics, or the idea that it is possible that politics dictate economics.

These are the concerns of a politician who knows that European integration is our common future, of a politician who tries to make sure that the result is the best one possible to achieve. Additionally, these are the concerns of a politician who expects that his country will become a full member of the

European Union in the near future, and that it will not wish to play an outsider's role there.

From a theoretical point of view, it is important to ask whether today's Europe is an "optimal currency area" (according to the definition by Robert Mundell), and if it is not, whether the ex-ante organized monetary unification will help to create such an area and, if so, at what cost.[1]

There is no doubt that the European Union is still characterized by the very heterogeneous structure of its member countries, and that today's 15-member European Union is not an optimal currency area. This heterogeneity is not an obstacle to lower forms of economic integration (such as the common market or customs union) but it is an obstacle to the emergence and smooth functioning of a monetary union — as we could learn from the collapse of the Czechoslovak monetary union, and from the politically motivated quick monetary unification of Germany. (If we go further back in history, we could speculate as to whether the monetary union of Italy in 1861 did not help to "freeze" the then-existent economic imbalance between the Italian north and south. In this respect, I am inspired by a recently published hypothesis on whether or not the former Socialist Germany could become a new Mezzogiorno.) At the same time, we must consider that there is a certain homogenization process, thanks to intended political-economic measures. The original European "Six" were definitely more homogeneous than today's "15" or the future's "20" or "27."

What are the reasons for the present structural heterogeneity among European states? What will its consequences be for the future monetary union and what could minimize its negative impacts?

1. There are several reasons for the heterogeneity of the economic structure of today's Europe:

First, there are natural differences in the *endowment of the individual countries* with factors of production, including such variables as weather, natural resources, access to the sea, etc. Because of that, the impacts of exogenous changes (= external shocks) are different in various economies. The existing differences, which I do not wish to (and cannot) analyze here, cannot be underestimated. Their existence is documented daily by the non-negligible tensions inside some countries of the European Union (for example, in the earlier-mentioned north and south of Italy). And this happens despite the fact that there is an undoubtedly stronger feeling of solidarity in these countries than there will be among countries in the future monetary union. I wish to add that this problem does not have the slightest connection with accomplishing the so-called Maastricht criteria.

Second, in Europe there are very different *"national propensities,"* traditions and habits that can hardly be changed considering their long-term historical anchoring; or to put it differently, their change in short- or middle-term is not possible (the other question is whether it is desirable). We could name a large number of examples of such national peculiarities, and the existing differences between countries will naturally be a source of future problems. Therefore, it can be predicted that the conflict concerning the extent and duration of transfers from rich to poor countries and from rapidly developing to stagnating ones will be permanent characteristics of the monetary union.

The third specific is something that would be possible to change, but that is in every moment "given," like the weather or the supply of gas. I speak of the *prevailing ideology* and resulting economic policies, I speak of a choice between the conflicting goals and of a choice of the *instrumentarium*, or intellectual tools, of economic policy. Europe is not homogeneous in either respect, and there has not been any "end of ideology," as Francis Fukuyama predicted. There are countries with right-of-center or left-of-center governments, political fights inside any country are irreconcilable — just like they have always been and always will be. The dreams of some European politicians that these problems will die off and that some non-politic or above-politic rationality will prevail are an example of one, very concrete and very well-known ideology. It is an ideology which I do not share. The priorities and preferences of various countries differ today, and they will continue to differ in the future.

2. These are — very simply formulated — starting preconditions for any serious discussion about the European Monetary Union. Introducing a single currency or transferring one economic parameter from the category of variables to the category of constants will mean:

- unequal impacts of world trade and its fluctuations (but also of other exogenous influences) on various countries without the chance of short-term and middle-term adjustments in nominal variables. As we all know very well, Maastricht convergent criteria do not include the economic growth or the dynamics of output, wages and employment. These variables will grow in various countries quite differently. The important thing is that their different developments will not lead to changes in the exchange rate, as it has up until now;

- the political unacceptability of growing differences in the economic level among countries will bring about the increase of transfer payments among countries and the centralization of budgeting. The solidarity of the Union will grow; the autonomy of fiscal policies and of decision-making authority will go down. It is legitimate that some of us may want this, some not. It would be naive to pretend that such a problem does not exist;
- the shift in decision-making structures will bring about a shift in the structure of basic political and constitutional institutions and it will mean a visible ideological change from traditional liberal (contractual) society to a more constructivist (and political) system. It is being discussed in Europe these days under the heading "democratic deficit."

3. Minimizing the negative impacts of the introduction of monetary union to a non-homogeneous area depends on the following two issues:

- on the degree of flexibility of the factors of production and their prices;
- on the degree of authentic European solidarity.

The monetary union will be easier to form if the mobility of the basic factors of production (labor and capital) is higher, even though there is no symmetry: "greater labor mobility is a cementing force of the union, while greater capital mobility is not."[2] The mobility of labor in Europe compared to America is much lower and, if I am not mistaken, no one in Europe is currently interested in increasing mobility among countries. I believe that none of us wish for "voting by feet," which means that a less-successful country would be increasingly depopulated and vice versa. If such a process is not to take place, there must be either an idyllic epoch of absolutely balanced, harmonic economic growth or an artificial coverage of differences by financial transfers from more successful countries to less successful countries.

Growing mobility of capital causes this problem to become more serious because capital follows success, not vice versa.

The same is true about price flexibility. The monetary union will be more difficult to organize, the more rigid prices of factors of production are. The price of labor is traditionally very rigid and I do not see any real chances to weaken the existing downward wage rigidity. Again, because I do not expect that, significant fiscal transfers will have to follow.

And that is how we come to my last idea. Again and again there is a question of fiscal transfers and European solidarity. The so-called cohesion fund founded by the Maastricht treaty represents an elementary form of the future European fiscal mechanism — with the only difference that it will be more costly. Every politician knows that a 1 percent increase or reduction of the share of GDP taken by the state budget inside a country leads to an occasional fall of government or to a change in election results. The idea that European taxes and European transfer payments will be excluded and put "in front of the brackets," that they will not be politically disputed, that they will stay away from standard political fighting, seems to me quite unrealistic and dangerous at the same time. The relationship between the individual and state, and any above-individual structure is a basis of political discussions in every democratic society and must not be changed in the future Europe. As a politician, I wish that I could decide on something "in front of the brackets;" as a citizen I wish to minimize such decisions.

I began my speech by saying that I consider the European Monetary Union the biggest postwar change, including the collapse of communism, in the Eastern part of Europe. We have to seriously discuss this issue, not only the final solution, but also the problems regarding the transition from one system to another. I hope that the debate about this will continue.

The Current European Challenge: The View from Prague

Barcelona, September 22, 1999

Europe is currently, at least nominally, preoccupied with two parallel processes: one of them is *the deepening* of the European integration process, the movement toward European unification, and the other is *the widening*, the expansion of the European Union to the East. I deliberately said "nominally" because, as I understand it, both processes do not represent the true interests, dreams and ambitions of European citizens. They are, both of them, advocated by several specific groups of European society only and are in the interest of one very influential rent-seeking group, the group of European bureaucrats, who are and will be visible net benefactors of both processes. There is no other "concentrated" group in Europe which could play the role of a countervailing power. With an uninvolved and indifferent majority of Europeans, who live in a nirvana of unconsciousness of what is going on and who maximize all pleasures coming from a relatively easy life in a mature, rich and in many dimensions "unconstrained" society which is unaware of its limits (and of its strong rivals and competitors), a small minority can have a decisive power.

I would like to say a few words about the European Monetary Union, but I have to admit that I am a very special person to talk about monetary unions, because I am well-known for dismantling a monetary union called Czechoslovakia. It gives me a very special perspective and a special sensitivity to this topic.

As a politician and a former economist, I have a frustrating feeling that everything about the EMU has already been said, that there is nothing to add, and that there is no lack of knowledge. The problem is whether we use the existing knowledge or not. Famous economists repeatedly tried to explain basic, more or less textbook arguments about both optimum currency areas and monetary unions, but I am afraid the architects of the EMU didn't listen carefully or sufficiently.

Well-known economists continue to remind us that the conditions for a successful monetary union are *microeconomic*, which means that they have directly nothing to do with the *macroeconomic* conditions specified at Maastricht. It has been repeatedly emphasized as well that the benefits of free trade are connected with a free-trade area and a customs union, and not with a monetary union. It has been argued that the appeal of getting something for nothing is wrong, that it is not possible to convert a variable into a constant without paying an inevitable price, without provoking movements of some other variable or variables.

I could go on with similar arguments, but it seems to me that it does not help because it became normal to talk about the benefits of a monetary union and not about its costs.

There will be costs and not just benefits. I will discuss here one issue only. It seems to me that the architects of the euro must be — to use labels well-known in the economic profession — new classicals or at least elasticity optimists. They have to assume that prices and wages in Europe are so flexible that exchange rate adjustment is not, and will never be, needed. Additionally, they have to assume that labor mobility is very high.

The empirical data do not support these assumptions. In such a situation, something else must become flexible. We call this variable fiscal transfers, but their potential size and frequency have not been seriously discussed. (All of us know that the size of fiscal transfers in a recently created monetary union called Germany was and still is enormous. I am aware of the size and frequency of fiscal transfers in a monetary union which used to be called Czechoslovakia. I was its last minister of finance, who was sending fiscal transfers from one part of the union to another, and I know that it was impossible to continue.)

When introducing the euro, it was — probably implicitly or subconsciously — assumed that currency domain (monetary union) can be greater than fiscal domain (fiscal union). As far as I know, it has never been proved, however, that this can be a viable institutional arrangement. I am convinced of the inevitability of the following path: monetary union → fiscal union → political union. One of the consequences of the EMU, and I include it on the side of costs, will therefore be the emergence of a fiscal and political union. And the justified question is: Do we really want a political union? I would strongly argue that we shouldn't feel guilty of a dreadful sin when we raise such a question, or even give a qualified answer to it.

The existence of a monetary union without political union means that countries delegate monetary policy to a supranational agency. It can be neutral only on the condition that there is a unified economic interest. It is, however, a very problematic assumption when we look at the current European heterogeneity. I'm afraid, therefore, that the costs and benefits of European monetary union will not be equally distributed among its members.

As regards the widening of the European integration process, my starting proposition is that the candidate countries — among them the Czech Republic — have a clear and straightforward interest: to participate in the European integration process, not to be left aside or behind, not to stay in a sort of vacuum. They have no real alternative to entry into the EU.

It should not be forgotten that entering the EU will be costly for them (as it has been costly even before entering). Their citizens are not sufficiently aware of it and they implicitly — and perhaps correctly — assume that it would be more costly not to enter. (To compare both types of costs together with their time structure is, nevertheless, difficult if not impossible.)

There are benefits connected with EU membership as well but they come with a delay and are less tangible than the costs. Nevertheless, this is what the citizens of these countries do not know. The candidate countries assume that the benefits are bigger than the costs.

Talking about interests, we should define who is on the other side. There is nothing like an EU interest. The EU does not behave in this respect as an entity. Only individual member countries have an interest (or interests). There is probably one exception. The bigger the EU, the bigger the political role and prestige of EU bureaucracy. As a result, *Brussels is more in favor of enlargement than individual member countries.*

The individual countries of the EU have *a much less clear interest* than the candidate countries:

- they know that they *do not have the right* to close the doors of their own distinguished club and to block other Europeans from entering it (it has, however, no relation to their genuine, down-to-earth interests);
- their interests are very *heterogeneous* (big vs. small countries, northern vs. southern countries, geographically more distant countries vs. countries close to new members, more agricultural vs. less agricultural countries, rich vs. less rich countries, etc.);
- the signing of association agreements between the EU and its future members together with their radical liberalization and widespread opening after the end of communism have led to a situation in which the existing EU members will not gain much from enlargement as compared to what they get now. (the "benefit" curves of members and candidates have different shapes);

- EU members are rationally or irrationally afraid of the costs of enlargement (because of inevitable fiscal transfers from various structural funds, because of the unpleasant problem of sharing farm subsidies, because of potential domestic employment problems caused by labor flows from new member countries, etc.).

We can say that the member countries assume that the costs of EU enlargement will be higher than the benefits.

The serious (and fair) question is the following one: *will the interests of both groups of countries — in the situation of asymmetric motivations — coincide?* I have to insist that to raise such a question is not an expression of defeatist Europessimism, that it is on the contrary an expression of responsible Eurorealism. The refusal to accept such a question is either Euronaivism or sheer hypocrisy.

Serious preparations (or homework) are unavoidable on both sides:

- future members must be able *to fulfill the Maastricht macroeconomic criteria* (with all accompanying consequences) and *to strengthen the microstructure* of their economies. They have *to harmonize* their legislation before entry;
- the EU has to make *institutional changes*; otherwise it will not be able to deal with more than 15 current members.

I do not want to speculate as to whose task is more difficult, but I challenge the dominant view that the unfulfilled tasks of the candidate countries represent the only existing obstacle to enlargement.

This brings me to my final point, which is the issue of the sustainability of current EU economic and social practices (and of the ideologies behind them). In my understanding the current system is, at least in the long run, untenable. The question is whether there is an easy way to change it — in an entity which has an undeniable democratic deficit as well as a non-negligible, geographically given, distance between individual citizens and politicians in Brussels.

We need *marginal, incremental, evolutionary changes* (and they will be — eventually — realized), but we need *more radical or revolutionary changes* as well. Europe (or the Euroland) has been in the past few decades a victim of *a creeping bureaucratization*, of *an increasing regulatory activism*, of *nonreceding protectionism* and of *soft and all-embracing paternalism* on the one hand, and of increasing *"planetary" ambitions* vis-à-vis "Le dèfi americain" or the Asian challenge on the other. Both processes are wrong.

European Integration or a European State?

New Europe Seminar on the Future of the European Union, Chatham House, London, January 10, 2001

For me (and for us in Central and Eastern Europe) the debate about the future of Europe has two crucial dimensions: the evolution of the type (or model or blueprint) of the European integration process and dealing with or perhaps *the absorption* of new members.

As someone from a nonmember country I have to argue that — unfortunately — membership or nonmembership in the EU has become a differentiating factor suggesting who is and who is not a "normal, standard (or standardized), mature, decent, obedient European" country. Despite the fact that it is unfair — for me difficult to swallow — it has been widely accepted. Because of that, we have no other alternative than to make a maximum effort to become members as soon as possible, regardless of our views about the currently realized model of European unification and the ideology behind it.

Speaking about EU enlargement, we live, however, in *the world of asymmetric motivations.* As I said, nonmembers are motivated to enter. However, I am convinced that it is of interest to member countries to prolong the status quo as long as possible. Rhetoric aside, they already have full access to the nonmember countries, they are there and have a full possibility to realize their own comparative advantages in a one-sided — for them painless — way.

As I see it, the only respectful ambition in Europe, which most of us would support, is to expand, enhance and guarantee freedom and democracy for the people of Europe. In this respect, the relevant question is the following: Will freedom and democracy in Europe be increased by:

- minimizing the role of one, undisputedly genuine and natural level of human organization, called "nation-state;"
- extending the distance between individual citizens and relevant decision-making bodies (regarding both legislative and executive powers);
- harmonizing (or unifying) rules and policies instead of preserving competition of different rules and policies?

To seriously tackle these questions is the only way to avoid aprioristic statements such as: Europe First, Down with Nationalism, etc. We all know that the issue is subtle and fragile and to answer the above-mentioned questions is not simple. It is nevertheless unavoidable.

I am deeply frustrated that these issues have not been seriously debated in Europe. A silent, uninvolved majority of Europeans do not care or do not see the importance of these issues. Pro-European activists — an apparent minority — claim to be the exclusive owners of truth. They dismiss all objections to their struggle for supranationalism and ever-closer union as undemocratic, nationalistic and reactionary, and denounce all those who disagree with them as potential Lukasenkos or Milosevics.

My answer to these questions is clear and straightforward:

- I wish my country to remain *a self-governing nation* within the European Union;
- I am convinced that it will be counterproductive to create *an artificial European state*;
- I hope that *the balance between intergovernmentalism and supranationalism* will not be fundamentally shifted;
- I believe that efficiency and strength will not come from *uniformity* but from *experimentation, diversity and competition.*

As regards the EMU, as an economist I have been, repeatedly, trying to argue that Europe is not an optimum currency area (in the standard economic definition). The arguments are well-known. It will have the following consequences:

- the costs of the monetary union will exceed its benefits;
- economically weaker regions, unprotected by changeable exchange rates and appropriate interest rates, will either be left behind or will require huge fiscal transfers;
- to realize such fiscal transfers will be impossible without fiscal unification;
- fiscal unification is impossible without political unification.

However, such unavoidable consequences of the EMU have not been explained to European citizens. It is our task to do so.

I have a very special expertise on monetary unions. I happened to be the last minister of finance of a dissolving monetary union called Czechoslovakia. And I know something about the inevitable fiscal transfers and about the impossibility of doing them without a strong political background. (Our original ambition was to keep the monetary union, but it collapsed in several weeks.)

Ten years ago we witnessed another monetary unification, called Germany. It was an artificial, not genuine unification. Costs have been enormous. (2000 fiscal transfers from Western to Eastern Germany exceed the Czech GDP.)

It reinforces my theoretical arguments and reservations.

The position of candidate countries is rather ambivalent. They need more flexibility than can be found in the straitjacket of the EMU (but perhaps not more than a Euroland country like Greece needs). They (like my country) are economically connected with Germany and are or will be very soon part of a German economic area whether they like it or not. They will be in a position like that of Austria or the Netherlands in the '80s and '90s.

The Czech Republic at the Gates of the EU

Business Leadership Forum, Instituto de Empresa, Madrid, March 4, 2002

Discussing Europe in March 2002, two parallel, directly unconnected issues should be analytically and strictly distinguished. The first one is the discussion of the process of European integration itself, of its forms, its speed, its phases, its costs and benefits, its spontaneous character and/or its political constructivism. The second one is the discussion of the possibilities of a small country, located in the heart of Europe, which was out of this process for half a century, to rationally participate in it. This is the issue of enlargement.

To openly discuss both issues is rather difficult, especially for a politician, because this is not a free, unbiased, non-aprioristic academic debate. The European intellectual space is dominated by one view which succeeded in caricaturing all other views as wrong, reactionary, nationalistic and undemocratic. This is very unproductive and can lead us to wrong ends.

Because of the unforgettable experience of my country with communism and — in this context — with the communist manipulation of words (in the true Orwellian sense), we are oversensitive to the methods and procedures used in the current European debate, and I suppose you may have similar feelings. My evaluation of the current stage of European integration — at least I hope — is based not on propaganda and wishful thinking, but on rational analysis and on the use of methods of economics and other social sciences.

The original foundation of European integration (as well as its consequent important turning points) has been a political act, not a spontaneous evolution of a social institution. It was projected as a human design; it was not a result of human action (to use Hayekian terminology). It has always been controversial because it was full of political ambitions. It has never been a technical, organizational or administrative issue; it was much more. It has its critics and its enthusiasts. It has its undisputable successes and its failures.

There are problems. The integration process doesn't address two main economic problems of our times: high unemployment and the expensive and demotivating welfare state. Its impact upon freedom is not clear either, looking at it from the European classical liberal tradition. We are witnesses of contradictory developments. I recently came across an old monograph entitled "Rome or Brussels?" published 30 years ago by the Institute of Economic Affairs in London.[3] These two cities already demonstrated the dual character of the EU, or, to put it differently, the contrast between its original motives and purposes and its current form, between its liberalizing and dirigistic character.

I believe that the original idea was to establish free trade, together with a free economy, in the territory of its members and that the optimistic hope was that more economic interdependency, as well as mutual economic improvement, would diminish political and economic tensions and would create closer union of the European peoples. The parallel, but — at the beginning — weaker and only supplementary idea was the retention and expansion of the European interventionist welfare state. If we ask which one of these ideas and tendencies is dominant now, I am afraid we have to answer that it is the second one.

We see it in the Common Agricultural Policy, in various nonviable development projects, in limits on competition and market pricing, in restrictions on the movement of people, in regulatory restraints on trade, commerce and business, in granting privileges to special groups, etc. It is not only a product of a hidden, creeping bureaucratization. It can be seen in the EU program documents as well, e.g., in the EU Charter of Fundamental Rights. The Charter contains some fundamental civil, political and economic liberties but, at the same time, interventionist and welfare state privileges and entitlements (in the role of trade unions, in labor legislation, in dismissal mechanisms, in the right to a life of dignity, in the right to participate in social and cultural life, in social security, in medical care, in unemployment compensation) which are considered "fundamental rights," instead of ideology-dependent forms of social policy.

Although communism is dead, the EU ideology — I call it Europeanism — prefers a system where increasingly the range of human action is becoming subject to collective, politicized procedures. It is based on the social market economy (*soziale Marktwirtschaft*) paradigm, on the idea of unification and harmonization instead of competition of legal and bureaucratic power structures and procedures. It is based on antifederalism (in the meaning of the federalist vs. antifederalist debate at the end of the 18th century) instead of competitive federalism (to some extent existing in the United States) — without taking into consideration the well-known arguments against supranationalism, e.g., in public choice theory (rational ignorance, voter apathy, etc.).

Paradoxically, the Single European Act of 1986, instead of producing free, competitive markets across Europe, "produced" harmonization and the so-called *acquis communautaire* which forces less-developed member states, and what is more dangerous, less-developed applicant countries, to adopt the more costly environmental rules as well as prohibitive welfare and working practices. This move was based on the belief that markets need the state, that more market must imply more state and that bigger markets require bigger states. Efforts are constantly being made to "standardize," "harmonize," or, in a different terminology, to rule, regulate and intervene. But Europeanizing government and bureaucracy does not mean unifying Europe.

A different issue is EU enlargement. Many people in Europe believe that a higher number of member countries means a less centralized and less unified Europe, but I think they are wrong. It will, instead, lead to accelerated unification, to further elimination of veto power and to "enhanced cooperation" (as it was named or renamed in Nice). It's considered to be a method for creating an *avant-garde* (Jacques Delors), or for making it possible for "a certain number of countries to show others the way" (Jacques Chirac). The EU Commission Report of July 1999 made it even more explicit; enhanced cooperation is prepared "not for those who want to reduce integration or extract themselves from certain policies."

I am convinced that regardless of their obligatory rhetoric, the member countries are interested in maintaining the status quo. The candidate countries are motivated to participate in European integration and to enter the EU. Their motivation is, however, not based on their excitement as regards the current model — which, as I suggested earlier, is a dualistic model — of the EU economic and social system. They historically belonged to Europe and believe that the only way to "belong" there again is to become EU member states. In addition, they have no feasible alternative for institutionally disconnecting themselves from their past. They know that they should not be the bridge between East and West because such a position led in the past to tragedies which they do not want to repeat.

They are afraid that their newly born and long awaited identity can be lost by far-reaching Europeanization. They have a historic memory full of experiences with the Habsburg monarchy, with Hitler's empire, as well as with Soviet imperialism and quasi-internationalism. The identity issue is there, is relevant, and should not be caricatured as an obsolete, long-defeated or overcome nationalism. We should not mix identity with culture because the applicant countries have always been European in the cultural sense of the word. If there ever was a need for some sort of cultural unification, this is happening regardless of formal membership. Identity means the possibility to control one's own destiny in a meaningful way, to have a sufficient degree of freedom for making one's own decisions (vis-à-vis external constraints or decisions from outside), and to have relevant political representatives within "reach" (whatever that means with current information and transportation technology).

It is fashionable now to argue that the word "distance" has become a meaningless concept, but that is just another modern fatal conceit. The fact that the spread of information and travel are faster than in the past may be an argument for world-wide integration (or globalization) of many human activities, for opening up, for enormously productive exchange of all kinds of human products (in a very broad sense), for more specialization and division of labor, but it means nothing as regards political architecture, freedom and viable democracy, as regards the concept of political representation and the relationship between individuals and the state.

This is what the ideology of Europeanism does not take into consideration or, perhaps, assumes away by implicit belief in the state or, what may be worse, by explicitly promoting the idea of the omnipotence of political and bureaucratic elites functioning at the continental level.

Too much attention in the contemporary Euro-debate about enlargement is paid to formal membership. The formal act is a relatively minor event as compared to all the events between the end of communism and the date of entry into the EU. The crucial moments were:

- the collapse of the communist closed society and the following far-reaching opening up of the countries in political, economic, social and cultural fields;
- their radical and historic transformation reflecting their own dreams and visions of a free society and aiming at creating a "normal" European economy and parliamentary democracy;
- their membership in other respected and important institutions and the compliance with their sometimes very demanding rules (IMF, World Bank, Council of Europe, WTO, OECD, BIS, etc.);
- signing association agreements with the EU and following the obligations connected with them;
- applying for EU membership and harmonizing legislation with the *acquis communautaire*;

- closing the so-called negotiating chapters, which implies accepting EU rules, norms, policies, etc.

The residual part between now and entry is rather small. By going through the above-mentioned steps, we gained enormously and became normal participants in all forms and fields of European relations, but at the same time, we paid very high costs which should be taken into consideration. But they are not.

Willingly, without being forced, we accepted many external recommendations and obligations because we ex-ante took identical or similar views: price and foreign trade liberalization, rapid privatization (IMF), democratic procedures (Council of Europe), trade liberalization (WTO), etc.

We had doubts about several recommended measures, but we accepted them as well: fixed exchange rate (IMF) and capital account liberalization (OECD).

Some of us, however, disagreed with the suggested ways of solving the current account deficit and averting the currency crisis (IMF), of dealing with a banking system heavily burdened by transformation (e.g., capital adequacy requirements — Bank of International Settlements), and of de-inflating the transition economy. We were aware of the huge costs connected with accepting such solutions but even that was done.

We are now in a different stage. Most of the past issues were policy issues, whereas the real trouble is the systemic one, reflected in the legislation and, specifically, in social, labor, environmental, safety, etc., standards or requirements imposed upon us by the EU.

The costs connected with them have two sources:

- some of them are associated with a very high stage of economic development and GDP (what is normal in the U.S. is not normal in India, and what is considered necessary in Denmark may not be relevant for Lithuania);
- some of them are part of a different ideology than prevails in countries with communist experience, especially with their distrust of masterminding society from above.

These "standards" deprive us of our comparative advantages and we see them as protectionist measures and costs (of non-negligible size). To our great regret, our arguments are not heard or are discredited a priori, which reveals the lack of sensitivity on the side of those who demand them.

The applicant countries need real convergence, need catching-up, need to make up for half a century of communism. The question is whether nominal convergence (the introduction of identical legislation and of single currency) helps to achieve real convergence or blocks it. The experiences of East Germany, of Southern Italy and to some extent of former Czechoslovakia tell us that premature nominal convergence creates problems. As a result, we live in an unfavorable constellation of "stars;" the benefits connected with the dismantling of communism, with liberalization and with our successful minimalization of inevitable transformation costs in the first stage of transition were matched with the costs of adjusting to EU standards. Some benefits connected with EU membership may arrive only after formal entry, not before it.

We care about the future of Europe (and of the West) no less than the people living in Western Europe care about it. But we understand more clearly the dangerous paradox of European unification: the belief in the possibility to preserve traditional European values when abolishing the original institutions that made the victory of these values possible. That is the reason for our Eurorealism and for our warnings against Euroapriorism.

Reflections on the Current Situation in Europe

Speech at the Mont Pelerin Society Meeting, Chattanooga, Tennessee, September 18, 2003

Here in Tennessee, my only comparative advantage is to speak about Europe. I see two main phenomena. First, the Central and Eastern part of Europe is in the second decade of its difficult transition from communism to a free society, and it finally understands that the transition is a costly and lengthy process. Second, Western Europe is — almost innocently and without realizing it — moving to a single European state. This project is based on a very dubious assumption that the more nominally unified the European continent is, the better. I will say a few words about both developments, but I will not discuss the recent disagreements between Europe and America about Iraq, or the artificially created dispute between the so-called old and new Europe.

1. Transition in Its Second Decade

The fall of communism in 1989 was followed by enormous expectations, not only in the former communist countries but also in the rest of the world. The reality could not satisfy them and we became more and more confronted with what I call the expectations-reality gap.

I am convinced that the reality is a success. It started with the surprisingly "velvet" way of eliminating the very nasty and oppressive totalitarian regime that had existed in our part of Europe for several decades. In my understanding, it was made possible by the growing weakness of the communist regime, which became soft (in dealing with its opponents) and visibly inefficient. Its ideology (system of beliefs) was quite unconvincing and nobody took it seriously. As a result, communism was not defeated. It more or less collapsed.

Some of our critics argue that the change was too velvet, which, however, is not my position. The whole transformation of the political, social and economic systems was done "live." Millions of people participated. It was not a controlled exercise in applied politics or economics. The politicians had to guarantee an elementary degree of functioning of the society, of the economy, of the administration and of the political system. More discontinuity (not to speak about anything approaching anarchy) would have been much more costly.

The reality has changed dramatically. The structure of society, the degree of political and economic freedom, the scope of government regulation, the quality of markets and the degree of openness of the economy have reached the levels of Western Europe.

Could the reality be much better? It undoubtedly could be. But we know that society is a complex system which cannot be masterminded from above. The transition from one system to another is not a laboratory experiment done in a vacuum but an interplay of millions of people who follow their genuine interests, who have political ambitions, and who are engaged in many forms of activities, including rent-seeking. The outcomes of the process of transition are, therefore, necessarily different from the reform blueprints.

The ambitious social planners of all kinds, colors and "isms" argue that they would have been able to do it differently. They suggest — now and then — doing it gradually, which means not liberalizing prices and foreign trade, not deregulating markets, not privatizing the economy. They probably have to assume that it would have been possible to convince the people to stop dismantling the old system and instead to start the decades-long process of institution and legislation building. It would require putting an end to political democracy and behavior based on genuine interests, and letting the well-minded interventionists prepare the legislation and institutions without the complications that arise with freedom.

I have problems with the misuse of the term "rule of law." The members of the Mont Pelerin Society know from Hayek and Mises that social institutions including law and its enforcement are a product of spontaneous evolution, of human action, not of human design. Social institutions are always imperfect and there is no way they would not be — at least not in a free society. To say that there is or is not "the" rule of law in one country or another is a very dubious statement.

The costs of transition (and of the dismantling of the old system because output began to collapse when the old system started to fail, not when transition began) have a strong negative impact upon many citizens who now support social democratic or socialist parties, who ask for more government intervention, who want more extensive social policy, who don't care about budget deficits, and who are more interested in strikes than in hard work. As a result, in most of the Central and East European countries the political parties advocating free markets are in the opposition.

Because of that and because of the impact of the EU we have not created a free capitalist system but a version of the European model of "social market economy" based on heavy regulation and on counterproductive welfare systems.

2. The impact of European unification and the attempts to create a post-political society

Several years ago I was arguing that in many respects we liberalized the economy more than Western Europe and that we should not accept the rigid and inefficient European economic and social model. We did not succeed. As you know, eight of the former communist countries were invited into the EU and in April 2003 signed the EU Accession Treaty. As one of the preconditions, we had to "take in" the complete body of EU legislation. It has changed our system for the worse.

Central and East European countries need economic growth and economic convergence with the old EU members, but I am afraid it is not attainable. The real convergence will not be made easier by nominal convergence (by entering the EU and by complying with EU rules and policies). On the contrary, the catching-up may be blocked or slowed down because of it. (The formal unifications both of Italy in 1860 and of Germany in 1990 do not suggest that nominal convergence helps. It was proved that in such a situation economic convergence was not possible without massive fiscal transfers, which are unavailable in the current EU.) It is not possible to rely on the long-term positive effects of the integration process, which was originally based on opening up and liberalizing trade. The current European integration process is more about regulation and new forms of intervention from above.

The draft of the EU Constitutional Treaty, prepared recently by the Convention for the Future of Europe, is a radical document with huge implications for the national sovereignty of individual European countries. The proposed constitution will create a new Union, separate from member states and with its own legal personality and status. The Union will derive its powers not from member states but from its own constitution, and its law will have primacy over the law of member states. Dual citizenship will be introduced. International treaty-making will be conferred to EU bureaucracy, etc.

It is a very problematic development. The attempts to denationalize citizenship represent a dangerous reinterpretation of human rights (not in the direction of a classical liberal political democracy). The attacks on the state (or on the nation-state) will — as the inevitable result — create a nonstate, but no one has yet proposed a democratic substitute for the nation-state.

Every treaty and summit takes Europe closer to such a brave new world. We have to ask whether the accelerated unification of the EU, the qualitative changes in the European integration process, ambitions which started in Maastricht, gained momentum in the 1990s, and reached their culmination in the current Convention on the Future of the EU — the shift from EC to EU, EMU, possibly EFU and EPU — will increase the welfare (however defined) of EU citizens, will promote the freedom and liberty in Europe, will improve the functioning of European society and its economy, and will enhance the position of Europe in the world. I am afraid it will not.

In the economic and social sphere, we are again witnesses to the disbelief in self-interest, in economic incentives, in the quality of the economic coordinating mechanism, in the price system. We are witnesses of the belief in promising fashionable or modern products, technologies or industries and of the belief that these can be masterminded by omniscient bureaucrats in government agencies. We face the same utopias as in the past, now in their computerized, digitalized versions. I am convinced that the counter-arguments are the same today as they were in the past.

We have to ask whether the European economy can survive the rigidities of the European labor market, the burdens of the European welfare state and the enormous size and scope of redistributive state activities, as well as the costs of bureaucratic regulation in all aspects of business. We have to ask whether the individual, very diverse European economies can benefit from the existence of a single currency, from the uniform monetary policy and from the absence of exchange rates among themselves.

My answers to all these questions are well-known and I believe they are mutually consistent. The problems I see in contemporary Europe have common roots — the misunderstandings of the causes of the Wealth of Nations, and the ideas and assumptions about the world that have come to prevail among large sections of politicians, social scientists, journalists and other opinion-makers in our countries. It has always been the role of the Mont Pelerin Society to fight them.

The European Constitution Will Change Our Future

Mlada fronta Dnes, October 16, 2003

When I heard several years ago about the idea of a European constitution, I hoped it was just the wishful thinking of European centralists and federalists and not a realistic project. For I wished, the same as a great part of Czech population, that the construction of the European Union would be based on nation-states and not individual citizens (the basic units of every democratic state). That is why I believed the constitution was not necessary.

Then a rather unexpected shift occurred. Following the general criticism of the tens of thousands of pages of chaotic European legislation, as well as of the unclear definition of the Union and its potential future development (incomprehensible for its citizens), some people began considering the idea of a brief document (that might be called a constitution), which would codify the basic relations of integrating Europe. It should clearly define the extent of such integration and set the limits to its development in the future. It might stop the creeping unification of Europe, which I was not the only one to criticize in the past and which has been — since the time of Jacques Delors — managed by the bureaucrats from Brussels behind the back of the continent's population, behind the back of the citizens of individual member states.

The so-called Convention, however, yielded a completely different result. Even though some Czech as well as European politicians still pretend it is a mere re-codification of the existing model of European integration and thus nothing to worry about (an opinion voiced in our country, for example, by the participants in the Convention negotiations, Jan Kohout and Josef Zielinec), the absolute majority of people who are really concerned know we have been confronted with a radical step: A step across the Rubicon which would be followed by the elimination of sovereign European states with their own governments and parliaments that represent the legitimate interests of their citizens in favor of the one state. Basic issues in such a state shall be decided by the distant "federal government" in Brussels and Czech citizens shall become a tiny particle, the voice (and influence) of which will be practically negligible. Yet there are some who welcome this prospect since that is the Europe they wish for.

We are to believe it is an "objectively" inevitable step and in fact a beneficial one. Yet, it is not inevitable because it is a result of a free decision made by human beings and not a law of physics. We have the right to accept or refuse it. If Europe did not maintain this freedom of decision, the situation would be really bad. Furthermore, such a step is not beneficial either. It will definitely weaken European democracy and deepen the "democratic deficit" existing in all supranational structures, and the advantages of a nation-state will disappear. The important elements of decision-making processes will be moved from Prague, Madrid or Helsinki to Brussels, the pressure for further unification (or harmonization) measures aiming at the artificial and unnatural uniformity of Europe (figuratively speaking, a search for a one-size suit to fit all, thin or fat, small or tall) will grow.

I certainly do not oppose European integration. I believe it will be beneficial if Europe reaches an agreement on the same road signs, the same import duties from third countries, the same labeling system of goods, and if European nations share the same cultural and civilization values (concerning capital punishment, organized crime, illegal trade with people and goods across borders, extremist movements, etc.). However, due to different economic levels, to the different stages of social development and to the cultural and political traditions of individual countries, it would be in fact harmful if we were to introduce uniform European "eintopf," if all were to have the same interest rates, taxes, social benefits, economic policy, foreign policy, the same share of domestic and foreign, European and American films on our televisions, closing hours for our shops, the same alcohol content in our beer and thousands of other things the same.

This is the core of the current debate about the European constitution. And still, this is what is often suppressed or underestimated. Many European governments (including our own, and particularly our Foreign Ministry) act as if the only problem to solve is the relative representation of individual countries in EU institutions. Yet, I am convinced that if we accepted this document as it stands today, if we remained silent or falsely loyal, we would participate in the decision to set off from the current crossroad of European history in the clearly federalist or even supranationalist direction.

We should all consider it again. And if we can define our own position, do not let us be shouted down as being anti-European. We may be against the European super-state but we may strongly support the emergence of a reasonably integrated, free and productive Europe.

The Future of the Euro: A View of a Concerned Outsider

Speech at the Cato Institute's "The Future of the Euro" conference, Washington, D.C., November 20, 2003

It is an enormous pleasure to be here today and to share the platform with so many distinguished scholars. I am afraid, however, that now, at the end of the conference, it is very difficult to come up with anything illuminating or surprising. In addition, I have the feeling that everything that is really relevant about the euro has been already stated (and accompanied by convincing arguments). The scarce factor is not the supply of arguments but the demand for them. It was, therefore, a very good idea of the Cato Institute to express its demand by organizing this conference and by inviting us to come here. It is frustrating not to have such meetings in Europe, where the arguments mostly remain at political or journalistic levels.

My own perspective is based on a special combination of three elements:

- my strong belief in the standard economic argument which is, in this field, summarized in the textbook theory of the optimum currency area;
- my citizenship in a small Central European country which in five months will be a new member of the EU and sooner or later a member of the European Monetary Union. I have an understandable personal interest in the existence of a rational and efficient monetary arrangement in my part of the world;
- my current political role, which forces me to openly reveal my position on my country's EMU membership.

My basic arguments can be summarized in the following way:

1. I am convinced that the driving force behind European monetary unification has been strictly political, not economic. This often-used argument can be supported by my own experience based on numerous explicit conversations about it with key European political leaders. The economic arguments have been marginalized or taken only very superficially. The political ambition has been quite dominant. The euro has always been considered to be a useful instrument for the creation of the European political union.

Many statements of that kind can be quoted. European President Romano Prodi made it quite explicit: "The introduction of the euro is not economic at all. It is a completely political step...The historical significance of the euro is to construct a bipolar economy in the world."[4] Two years before that he said: "the two pillars of the nation-state are the sword and the currency and we changed that."[5] Gerhard Schröder in March 1998, still an opposition leader, said that "the euro is a sick premature infant, the result of an over-hasty monetary union." After eight months as German Chancellor, he made a different statement: "Our future begins on January 1, 1999. The euro is Europe's key to the 21st century. The era of solo national fiscal and economic policy is over." Spanish Prime Minister Felipé Gonzales said in May 1998: "The single currency is a decision of an essentially political character...We need united Europe. We must never forget that euro is an instrument for this project." I can quote indefinitely but the words will be almost the same.

2. I believe that the largest part of the positive economic impact of European integration (as well as of EU enlargement) has come through the liberalization of trade and investment and has already been obtained. The marginal contribution of further economic or noneconomic unification will be close to zero, if not negative. Because of that, the birth of the euro as well as the day of the next EU formal enlargement in 2004 do not represent any breakthroughs. I agree with Patrick Minford that "trade patterns are determined by comparative advantage, not by monetary factors" and that the role of the exchange rate risk as a factor determining foreign investment and the cost of capital is relatively small.[6] Trade does not need to have the same currency on both sides of the transaction.

3. To look at the economic performance of the euro-zone in the first years of its existence, even the pro-European activists must admit that the overall expectations of an economic boost and the claims that the introduction of the euro would speed up economic growth have not been fulfilled. This is not a surprise for me and, to be fair, not everyone had such expectations. Rudiger Dornbusch, a man who was always sharp and consistent and whom we miss very much, wrote in 1996 that "EMU moved from an improbable and bad idea to a bad idea that is about to come true." Many of us knew then and know now that the formation of a regional common currency is neither a necessary, nor a sufficient, condition for healthy economic growth. It seems, on the contrary, that the Europeans have imprisoned themselves in a rigid monetary arrangement, which led to a loss of a non-negligible part of their originally existing flexibility.

When we look at the current European monetary and overall economic problems, we have to — at least analytically — differentiate between two issues: one is the impact of a monetary union upon nonidentical countries, but countries that are at a similar level of economic development, another is the impact of entry into a monetary union of a country which is at a different level of economic development than the dominant part of the union and which is undergoing dynamic structural changes in an effort to catch up with its more-developed partners.

4. The costs and benefits of a monetary union differ among similar but nonidentical countries. The conditions formulated four decades ago by Robert Mundell, in 1961, as regards the optimum currency area are well known.[7] Their fulfillment guarantees a favorable balance between costs and benefits of a monetary union; their nonfulfillment does not. They include:

- the sufficient extent of labor mobility among parts of the monetary union;
- the lowest possible degree of wage rigidity inside individual countries;
- similar factors of production endowments and a symmetry of exogenous shocks and impulses;
- the existence of an adequate fiscal compensation mechanism.

These conditions are currently not fulfilled in Europe. Labor mobility in Europe is — as compared to other monetary unions — relatively very low and the required downward wage and price flexibility is almost nonexistent. The rigidities of the European labor market are well-known and well-documented, which is in contradiction with the basic requirement, which says that where labor markets do not function well, flexible exchange rates are all-important.[8] The asymmetric shocks and impulses appear again and again, which is not surprising because the euro-zone countries are different. The size of fiscal transfers at the EMU level is, however, very small. There exists some international solidarity among EU members but its level cannot be compared to the solidarity in nation-states.

The assumed benefits — the reduction in transaction costs and of exchange risk — will be in reality rather small. With the current level of financial and banking sophistication, transaction costs are saved only in tourist transactions, not in other fields.

I agree with Irish economist Anthony Coughlan that, "the economic advantages of being able to travel within the euro-zone without having to change currency, and of being able to compare prices more easily between euro-zone countries, are small compared to the economic disadvantages."[9] I especially agree with his argument (which I myself use quite often) that "people may be on holidays in other euro-zone countries for two or three weeks a year, but they have to be working for the remaining 48-49 weeks at home." The above-average benefits can be gained exclusively by the permanently traveling EU politicians and their bureaucrats.

We should not forget that joining the euro does not mean joining a world currency but only a regional one where the exchange risk basically remains. It does not mean, of course, that I would suggest creating a world currency along the lines of recent suggestions by Robert Mundell, as described by Herbert Grubel.[10]

The costs of monetary unification are important. They include the loss of independent monetary policy, which mostly means the loss of interest rate-setting power and the loss of the possibility of exchange rate movements. When I say this, it is not as an advocate of the policy of competitive devaluations. I don't, however, believe that European economies have sufficient alternative flexibility to avoid problems resulting from such a rigid parametric structure. To eliminate two important policy variables — interest rates and exchange rates — means either to rely on a textbook level of perfect microflexibility or to be prepared for large fluctuations in the real economy, or to expect the acceleration of fiscal transfers inside the monetary union.

Such perfect microflexibility does not exist. The sluggishness of domestic prices and wages forces the exchange rate to be the shock absorber, which is not the same as competitive devaluation. It is easier, stresses Bob McTeer, "for your exchange rate to adjust to your economy and policies than for your economy and policies to adjust to a predetermined exchange rate."[11] (Coughlan's arguments seem to be persuasive: "the years 1993-99 were the only period in the history of the Irish state that it pursued an independent currency policy and allowed the exchange rate to float...The intelligent use of an independent currency is the principal reason for the Irish economic boom, which has attracted such international attention in recent years."[12])

I would like to mention two other phenomena which I put on the side of costs. A single currency (without fiscal unification) creates an environment for fiscal irresponsibility. We can even talk — together with Anthony de Jasay

— about fiscal free-riding: "Each member state of the euro-zone is caught between two alternatives — to engage in fiscal free-riding or to be the victim of free-riding by the others."[13] In the same spirit Peter Kenen rightly asked in 1996 whether the currency domain can be bigger than the fiscal domain.[14] I don't think it can. When a country has its own currency, fiscal irresponsibility carries its own punishment. Such punishment does not, however, exist in the current euro-zone. The fiscal deficits in some of those countries after the establishment of the euro seem to support this argument.

In addition, European monetary unification is the Trojan horse for overall harmonization of economic rules, policies and laws in the EU. I am convinced that any euro-zone problem in the future will be interpreted as a consequence of the lack of harmonization (of nominal unification) and will lead to another wave of creeping harmonization. Hans Eichel, the German minister of finance, made it quite clear: "The currency union will fall apart if we don't follow through with the consequence of such a union. I am convinced we will need a common tax system."[15] Such an unnecessary and counterproductive harmonization (and centralization), which tries to eliminate the comparative advantages of individual countries, is one of the most worrying elements of the whole European integration process.

Comparing the above-mentioned costs and benefits, I am afraid that it is not true that the costs of the European monetary unification do not exceed the benefits. They do. Sluggish economic growth in Europe since the introduction of the euro is not proof of that, but it is not an accident either.

5. There are costs and benefits connected with the entry into a monetary union of a transition country which needs real, not only nominal, convergence.

Eight Central and East European countries will become EU members in May 2004 and in their accession treaties with the EU, signed in April 2003 in Athens, they promised to enter the euro-zone.

Many people in these countries look forward to it. They expect to gain from euro stability, from decreasing the exchange-rate risk, from a credible monetary policy. I am struck that they don't see the other side of such an arrangement because it is more than evident that the transition countries need a maximum of flexibility and should not introduce any artificial rigidities. They should not take actions against their own economic interests for political reasons.

The main costs for them will be the loss of independent monetary policy, which should be — for the countries in transition, for the countries undergoing radical structural changes, for the countries at a lower level of economic development — visibly different from the policy of the developed and more stable EU member countries of Western Europe. It makes no economic sense for them to have the same interest rate as Germany or France (not to open another topic — the fact that ECB is not subject to any democratic control and has a deflationary bias in its policy).

The same importance has for them the loss of the possibility of exchange rate movements. Transition countries are in a permanent process of real appreciation and there is no way to make it possible with fixed exchange rates, with the inflation and interest rate targets of the Maastricht Treaty, and with the Stability Pact conditions concerning budget deficits. There is an additional danger that there will be a very high risk of fixing the exchange rates away from long-term equilibrium because the convergence process will not be — in the moment of their entry into the euro-zone — completed. The result will be the insufficient final exchange rates realignment (the problem we see with current euro-zone members as well).

I repeat that I am not an advocate of misusing exchange rate movements for competitiveness reasons. I myself at the end of 1990 radically devalued the Czechoslovak crown (but not in an attempt to gain competitive advantage) and immediately after that introduced a fixed exchange rate regime. I was afraid of setting an unsuitable exchange rate level, but the belief in the use of the exchange rate as an anchor for stabilizing inflation was then overwhelming. I was aware of creating a dangerous rigidity that would constrain future responses to internal and external pressures and impulses and tried to find an optimal moment for abandoning such an arrangement. I have to admit, however, that I did not find it (the floating of the Czech crown in the spring of 1997 came too late).

But such an exchange rate-based stabilization of inflation is not our current task. The rate of inflation is very low and we need flexibility in nominal variables, not their rigidity. One clever Czech economist, then-Deputy Minister of Finance Miroslav Koudelka, made a point 35 years ago which I still remember: "when everything is frozen, you may go skating but you cannot run a rational economic policy." It was an argument used in the Czechoslovak economic reform debates in the '60s and I believe it is valid now as well.

Rigidities of a monetary union and a growing implicit macroeconomic disequilibrium will block real convergence and will create "transfer economies" (like East Germany after reunification), which will be, however, forced to exist without adequate fiscal transfers because they are — in the contemporary EU — not available.[16]

My conclusion is that there is no need for these economies to rush into the Euro-zone.

6. The future of the euro: The euro is here and it is here to stay. I do not expect its end, even if I know that it is relatively easy to dismantle a monetary union. My own experience with the termination of the Czechoslovak monetary union in February 1993 suggests that it can be done without serious costs, smoothly and efficiently.

I expect, however, that to keep the European single currency will be costly in terms of economic growth and in terms of inevitable fiscal transfers aimed at compensating the weaker partners. It may even generate unnecessary tensions among nations. We should be aware of it.

Implications of the Recent EU Enlargement: An Attempt at an Initial Analysis

IFO Conference — Institute for Economic Research, Munich, June 22, 2004

During recent weeks, we could read hundreds of statements about the historic significance of the EU's enlargement by 10 new members, mostly former communist countries of Central and Eastern Europe. Many words were uttered. I am afraid, however, that there were very few serious, correctly structured analyses.

The *a priori* approach of practically all of the speakers and commentators stressed that enlargement would be a definite positive change, beneficial for all. Nevertheless, any consideration of this affirmation, any criticism, questions or reminders of non-zero costs of this change were considered as shortsighted or malicious intent. It was resolutely refused, caricatured and depreciated.

I must start by mentioning one seemingly irrelevant matter. A considerable number of statements and commentaries focused on the enlargement of Europe (and not the European Union). It was very painful and outrageous for the new member states because they understood very well that it was not a slip of the tongue. They cannot cope with it. Countries like the Czech Republic were in the past, are now and will be European in the EU as well as outside of it. They were European before the EU existed and will be European after any future metamorphosis of the order of the European continent. Hence, no single concrete, time-conditioned form of European order ever had or has the right to appropriate the term "Europe." To identify Europe with the European Union is a methodological error, and displays a lack of humility toward history and at the same time an extraordinary insensitivity that we should not commit.

In my brief speech, which is not a political statement of the president of a new member country, but rather a speech of an academically thinking president in an academic environment, I cannot attempt to perform a scientific analysis of this year's EU enlargement, let alone conduct an empirical analysis. This remains a long-term task for academics. Even for them, it will not be an easy goal, because we do not possess any adequate scientific methodology or instruments properly attuned to the task. Therefore, I will at least attempt today to outline the elementary structure of the problem by distinguishing the consequences of enlargement for the new member states, for the old member states and for the EU as a whole.

1. Consequences of formal membership for the new member states

At the very moment of entry — though it is an entry with many exceptions and restrictions (which represent advantages for existing members) — the new member countries acquire certain, for them extremely important, political recognition. They receive formal confirmation of the high level of their political, economic and civilizational maturity, advancement and stability. After half a century of abnormality, half a century of life in communism, membership in the EU makes it possible again to include them among normal, standard European countries. This acknowledgement is of utmost importance for these countries and their citizens. This is also the principal gain for them out of the EU membership, although not everyone knows that this gain is rather symbolic and has no immediate tangible effect. These countries have worked for this acknowledgement for 15 years. In a certain way, their membership in the EU — for themselves and for the "rest of the world" — is a sign that the era of the post-communist transformation is terminated once and for all and that they are now countries with the same systems and institutions as Western European countries. So they have the same system and institutions as countries that were lucky enough not to be an object of communist experiment. I do not see many other immediate effects. Usually we hear about the effects of the opening, the effects of the liberalization of the movement of persons, goods, capital and especially ideas. However, the size of the opening of these countries to EU countries, and the other way around as well — the opening of EU countries to these countries — did not change in any way after May 1, 2004. The effects of mutual intensive relations have been gradually growing since the fall of the Berlin wall and the cropping of barbed wire of the Iron Curtain in November 1989. These effects were "consumed" long before May 1, 2004. The residual effect of formal membership, from the perspective of relations among countries and from the perspective of relations among their individual subjects, is and will remain very small.

The direct financial effect is marginal as well, primarily for the more advanced countries among the new members. It seems that the Czech Republic will be in the near future a net payer and not a net receiver of EU money, which is very different from the status quo of the time when countries like Greece, Ireland, Spain or Portugal joined the EU (or rather the EC at that time). For this reason, it is not correct to name these countries as examples. Indeed, many citizens of the new member states believed in the experience of these economically less-advanced countries and they were expecting the same. That will not be the case.

I do not see any important effect in the fact that the new member states could obtain the possibility of influencing the decision-making processes within the EU. They are not sufficiently prepared for it; they will remain in the role of "junior members" for a long time. The overwhelming majority of them are small countries and the most serious obstruction is the EU's democratic deficit and its present scale of bureaucracy, which really makes their effective participation impossible anyway.

The new member states adopted the EU legislation, the so-called *acquis communautaire*, before their accession, and together with it also the European (originally German) model of a corporativistic state, *soziale Marktwirtschaft* — unambiguously associated with little competitive strength of companies, inflexibility and rigidity of the economy, high unemployment and slow economic growth. These countries, on a lower-than-average economic level of the European Union, will not be conduced to a real economic convergence. There even exists a threat that this nominal convergence (the adoption of EU legislation) will, on the contrary, slow down the real convergence. There is absolutely no need to overplay this fact in the country which experienced *Vereinigung* (or "combination"), where the effects of reunification (or, in other words, a rapid nominal convergence) are well known. However, it must be said that in this sense, even the first of May 2004 itself does not bring any fundamental change, because the EU legislation had been adopted for many years, or more precisely, its adoption was the prerequisite and not the consequence of the entry.

This outline of positive, neutral or negative effects, respectively, certainly is neither exhaustive nor sufficiently empirically-based, but I believe that it can be an inspiration and a starting point for a deeper analysis. However, I must insist that it is based on the real experience of an active participant in the preentry era, that it is not a view of an independent observer.

2. Consequences of EU enlargement for the old member countries

Even though the effects of the asymmetric preentry liberalization and the ingenuous opening for future member states represented a clear advantage for the more advanced, older member states, I have the feeling that the formal membership of the new member states is not any effective advantage for the old member states. Despite the fact that the gain from contacts with these countries was superior to the costs during the whole preentry era for the old member countries, after having achieved formal membership, the proportion of costs and benefits of contacts with the new members changes for the worse. The old member countries are aware of this and that is why they were not rushing with their consent for EU enlargement. I am not resentful, because I respect authentic human interests. It is not by any means a surprise, that it was the Brussels bureaucracy who pushed enlargement (bureaucracy always tries to extend its territory of coverage) so much more than the old member countries. I repeat that I consider their attitude rational and therefore, there is no reason for them to contest it. In consideration of the — indeed wrongful, but recurrent — identification of the EU with Europe, the old member countries could not preserve the exclusiveness of the EU club any longer and therefore the enlargement happened — without reference to the real interests of these countries.

It is very difficult to analytically separate the effects of very close relations between the old and the new member states existing for more than a decade, i.e., before the EU enlargement, from the effects that have emerged after enlargement. The competition for EU money is certainly going to grow. It is for sure that migration will augment — probably less than expected — the migration of manpower (but also of students) towards richer countries. Definitely, some Western Europeans will only now "find the courage" to go to the new member countries for the first time as tourists, businessmen or investors. Definitely, cultural and civilizational exchange in general will be reinforced. But these phenomena are difficult to quantify. For this reason, I do not dare to present any tentative quantitative estimates of the consequences of these effects. However, we should not produce cheap propaganda the other way around.

In sum, we can say that the immediate effect of this year's enlargement will not be significant for the old member states and that this effect will be difficult to observe and to analyze quantitatively.

3. Consequences of EU enlargement for the EU

Increasing the number of members from 15 to 25 signifies the expansion of the EU as an institution. By emphasizing the word "institution," I would like to suggest that it does not mean a clear expansion of the single market, because this expansion became true long before the moment of the formal enlargement. At the same time, it is certainly true that little manpower mobility, rigidity of economic relations and administrative complications, which are typical for the EU, were not essentially modified after May 1, 2004. Thus, the quality of the market has not changed.

This year's enlargement will conduce to exaggerate illusions of those with a "bloc," or perhaps a continental, vision of the world, that is to say, of those people who suppose that a bigger and more compact Europe will have a better chance of facing U.S. hegemony and Asia's enormous aspirations. This bloc (or "blocistic") vision of the world that is so clearly shown in the project of the European Constitution is a fatal error. Europe is (and will remain for a long time) a mere conglomerate of countries, and we cannot in any case talk about the authenticity of the European "people." In addition, no evidence exists to prove that "big is beautiful." Even European competitiveness is only a statistical artifact, because the competitiveness of a continent does not exist; only companies can be said to be competitive or not. Neither the continent nor the EU is an economic subject; it does not produce, does not trade, does not innovate, does not invest, does not economize, does not redeploy production and does not reduce costs. This blocistic vision of the world, which continues to expand in politics and the media, is in sharp contrast not only to the political, economic and demographic realities of contemporary Europe, but also to dominant globalizing tendencies.

EU enlargement to 25 members does significantly affect the decision-making process in the EU. There will be an increase in transaction costs for the functioning of this institution, as ten countries are added to the existing mechanism without any change therein (corresponding to a 40 percent increase). This is the price for the enlargement, but its amount is not easily quantifiable. Consequently, it is understood only a little and discussed with little seriousness. The volume of policies, activities and interventions in the EU is not declining (the adoption of the constitution in its current form should entail, on the contrary, a radical increase) and it has — with the increase in the number of participating subjects — nonzero costs. That applies for every centralized and hierarchically organized system, and it is a regularity which cannot be avoided.

There still exists one method of reducing these transaction costs (or rather slowing down the increase). It is reinforcing the democratic deficit of decision-making, reducing the volume of democratic procedures for the sake of hierarchic decision-making, increasing the power-sharing of the EU's narrower core, increasing the number of areas where majority vote is being applied, etc. Without a doubt, accruement of anonymity in decision-making, continuing the aggrandizement of distance between the citizen and the decision-making center and continuing the depersonification of the EU as such also belongs in this category. These are in any case evidently negative consequences of the recent EU enlargement. Unfortunately, they are not reversible by the good intentions of politicians or bureaucrats.

In order to be understood correctly, I will repeat my argument. We have three variables: the number of member states, the scope of EU policies and the mechanism of the decision-making process. There is not and could not be a positive complementarity among those, but rather a tradeoff, tit for tat. Increasing one variable (the number of countries), with the unchanged second variable (volume of policies), will necessarily cause the third variable (decision-making mechanisms) to adjust. I have to insist that to pronounce this trivial conclusion is not Euroskepticism, but the use of elementary logical thinking. And it is our obligation to do just that.

Herewith, I get to draw conclusions. The formal EU enlargement does not represent any radical change. It is only a starting point for the reinforcement of processes that have been in progress with variable intensity during the last decade. Some had positive marks, others had negative marks, and it will remain the same in the future as well. I see the basic problem in something else. I see it in an indispensable change of the essential order of the prevailing European communitarian model. A year ago, Europe was being divided into the old and the new, according to a criterion of preference on the way to promote political and civic freedom in the world. I do not consider this a useful and fair division. Let us try to keep the term "New Europe." Let us try to give it the significance of a Europe of economic freedom, a Europe of small and non-expanding government, a Europe without state paternalism, a Europe without pseudo-moralizing political correctness, a Europe without intellectual snobbism and elitism, a Europe without supranational, all-continental ambitions, a Europe without the ideology of Europeism. If somebody across the ocean should label this kind of a Europe with the expression "New Europe," it would only be good. However, I must emphasize that the recent EU enlargement of 10 new states will not have these implications.

Address of the President of the Czech Republic Delivered on the Eve of the Accession of the Czech Republic to the European Union

Spanish Hall of the Prague Castle, Prague, April 30, 2004

Dear guests, my fellow citizens:

In a few hours we shall become witnesses of, as well as participants in, one of the most important events in the history of the Czech state. When I speak about history, I mean those one thousand years of our existence, not only the relatively short period of our modern statehood since January 1, 1993. Tonight at midnight the Czech Republic will cease to exist as an independent state and will become a part of the European Union

This event is not unexpected for any of us. It has been planned for a long time and it had several preliminary stages. Already in November 1989 hundreds of thousands of us — almost subconsciously and thus completely spontaneously — coined a slogan "Back to Europe," a slogan that became one of the most important symbols of our further development. It became a challenge to:

- overcome the isolation of our country that lasted half a century;
- overcome our unnatural and one-sided orientation towards the East;
- end our disrespect for the basic values of the political and economic systems functioning successfully west of us; and
- end our noninvolvement in the activities of those European institutions that had been founded during our absence from the democratic development of the free part of the European continent between February 1948 and November 1989 and that shaped the face of today's Europe.

We have accepted this challenge and the result is today's accession into the European Union. In this respect, this day is the end of the last one-and-a-half decades. It was made possible by cutting the barbed wire on our borders in the last days of November 1989. It was connected with the birth and gradual maturing of our democracy and with the implementation of the values of a free society in our country. It was prepared by our radical transformation measures, first of all by opened borders enabling not only the free movement of people but also of ideas, which was followed very soon by the liberalization of trade (that allowed the free movement of goods and services over the borders) and, last but not least, by the liberalization of financial transactions which opened our country and our economy to Europe and to the world. It was repeatedly confirmed by our membership in many regional, European and global institutions — in the North Atlantic Alliance, in the Council of Europe, in the International Monetary Fund, in the Organization for European Security and Cooperation, in the Organization for Economic Cooperation and Development, in the Central European Free Trade Zone, in the *Visegrád* group and in many others. It was accelerated by our association with the Union in October 1993 and by our application for full membership in January 1996. And it was based on our domestic activity linked to the radical reconstruction of our political, economic and social system. The uneasy last years marked by massive transposition of the European Union legal system were the final culmination of this process.

As it is usual in the lives of individuals as well as of the whole human society, we will gain something today, but at the same time we will lose something. We never get anything for free. We should do everything to make sure the proportion of gains and losses is favorable for us, which certainly is not and will not be automatic. It will depend on us. The terms and rules relevant today for all European Union member states as well as the specific conditions we ourselves have negotiated prior to our accession (and there is no point now arguing whether they are optimum or not) are a reality we cannot change. We must learn to move among them. We must learn how to realize ourselves not only as individuals but as a Czech nation which is more than the sum of individual interests. These wider interests do exist and let us not allow anyone of us or anyone outside even for a second to label them as nationalism. We are obliged to our predecessors to preserve Czech statehood. We must not join the European Union as individuals or various institutions, communities, municipalities or regions. We are joining the European Union as the Czech Republic.

The exceptional quality of this historical moment will motivate speakers here as well as abroad to deliver lofty speeches about Europe, about Europeism, about European civilization and culture and about the values that have been applied on this continent for centuries — surely in a slightly different manner than in other parts of this world. It will motivate them to poetry. And I would like to warn against it. We are not joining Europe; indeed, we have been part of it for a long time now, in fact always, even at the times of our subjugation.

We are joining the European Union and our task is thus much more prosaic: We must learn how to live in the structures of Brussels and in the complicated supranational organization which has nothing to do with poetry. We must not get lost there. We must make sure that our identity does not get blurred and that we do not lose the basic attributes of the Czech state which — I firmly believe — we all respect and shall respect also in the future.

I am an optimist. And thus I am convinced that, judged by our past as well as by our future, we shall succeed in our task, in the task of the current generation, and that we shall use this extraordinary moment in a positive way.

European Problems and Their Nonsolutions

Speech in the U.K. House of Commons for the Burges Group, London, October 20, 2004

When discussing Europe now, at the beginning of the 21st century, I must confess that I am more and more nervous — both because of what the discussion includes and because of what it is missing. It has become more or less accepted that all the fundamental questions of our times have been solved at some point in the past and that history is over. Almost all participants in the discussion pay exaggerated attention to — for me — the minor issues. In the contemporary brave new world, where online reporting and SMS-length headline news predominate, everyone behaves as if the real issue in Europe is about whether or not to invite three more states to join the EU, whether to have a rotating or permanent EU presidency, whether to have more or fewer commissioners in Brussels, and whether to have one system of majority voting or another.

I am afraid that such topics are of second-rate importance, that they do not address the main European problems and — what is even worse — that those who formulate them succeed in crowding out all other topics. We should do something. We should not capitulate to the intellectual trends of the time. We should raise our concerns. The European intellectual space should not be occupied by topics relevant for EU politicians and bureaucrats only, for a group of people someone recently aptly called the "priviligentia."

One need not have extraordinarily sharp eyes to see in recent developments in Europe evident, non-deniable and undoubtedly unfavorable trends and tendencies. These include:

- a long-term economic slowdown (both in relative and absolute terms);
- the growing success of various radical political parties and of nationalistically or populistically oriented movements;
- the loss of cultural dynamism coinciding with the victory of multiculturalism and a belief in the possibility of preserving traditional European values when abolishing the original institution that made them possible;
- the loss of self-confidence, of a positive work ethic and habits, and of personal motivation;
- the breakdown of the understanding of the inevitable performance-reward nexus;

- a growing short-sightedness connected with an unconscious and unstructured fear of the future;
- loss of leadership, the depersonification of decision-making in the public sphere, the shift to collective (ir)responsibility;
- the growing disbelief in politics and in politicians at the moment when an increasing range of human actions is becoming subject to collective, public choice procedures;
- the undermining of national identity and (because the search for identity has been caricatured as an obsolete, long-defeated nationalism) the emergence of symptoms of new nationalism.

I do not think these phenomena have any direct connection with either the recent enlargement of the EU or with the birth of the EU constitution. To my great regret, the new members from Central, Eastern and Southern Europe have not and will not bring about an important change because most of them have already been — between the collapse of communism and their entry into the EU — infected by the same virus. The countries from more remote regions could bring some new air, but if such a threat arises, they would not be allowed to enter.

The recent enlargement of the EU will have a different impact. Because everything will be bigger and more complicated the inherent failings of the current EU system will increase and become more visible:

- both the democratic deficit and the lack of democratic accountability of EU institutions will be more apparent than before;
- the composition of decision-making procedures will further shift from a democratic type to a hierarchical one;
- the power of the EU "core" will be strengthened;
- majority voting instead of unanimity will dominate decision-making in more and more fields;
- attempts to get rid of existing deviations from the "norm" will lead to more intervention from above;
- the distance of citizens from the center of power, from Brussels, will grow;
- the anonymity of decision-makers will increase.

All of that is — given the prevailing integrationist goal of building an "ever closer union" — unavoidable. The unpleasant trade-off between the number of participating countries and the democracy and efficiency of decision-making (all other things being equal, *ceteris paribus*) will be felt more and more. The costs of decision-making in a bigger union will either be paid for (resulting in a loss of efficiency) or suppressed and hidden (resulting in loss of democracy). Both have a negative sign.

The recently approved and soon to be signed European constitution (or perhaps constitutional treaty) will increase both types of costs. In its current form it is a radical document with far-reaching consequences for freedom, for the welfare of individual citizens and for the future of nation-states. Somebody may argue that this all sounds too alarmist and that we are not that far yet. This is true. All that is required, however, is one more treaty. This is my forecast, not a wish.

The new constitution does nothing to resolve the real problems of Europe and tries to sidestep them instead. I dare to say that it was caused either by an intellectual defect or by a purposeful and skillfully planned intention.

Whatever the reason, the authors of the constitution started with very dubious assumptions:

- Europe existed in the past as a collective identity and should, therefore, exist as a collective identity in the future again;
- Europe has a common history which can be — as with national history — implanted into human minds by means of fairy tales, textbooks, preachings and political speeches;
- the gains from homogenization of the whole continent, from the elimination of differences, from the harmonization and standardization of the rules of human behavior are indisputable;
- competition is not the most powerful mechanism for achieving freedom, democracy and efficiency, but rather an unfair and unproductive form of dumping which endangers specific protected groups and, eventually, whole societies;
- big is beautiful and centralization, bureaucratization and masterminding of the whole continent will make us stronger;
- intrusive regulation, ruling and intervening from above are necessary because market failure is more dangerous than government failure, because markets need the visible hand of omnipresent administrators to be efficient, and because bigger markets require more regulation;

- regulators at the EU level are better, more efficient, less inclined to listen to special interests than their colleagues at the national level, or to put it differently, the more remote (from individual citizens) the government is and the bigger the territory it governs, the better the government is.

I do not share these views. I do not believe in this conglomerate of ideas characterized by extreme elitism and lack of consistency and purity. I call this conglomerate of ideas — for want of a better term — Europeanism.

Its incoherent structure makes it possible to see it as a proof of the end of ideology, of the victory of pragmatism as well as of administrative and technical reasoning, of the importance of genuine and friendly interest-free (which means altruistic) cooperation, of the possibility of win-win solutions (which is a term that surpasses all the terminological inventions of George Orwell), etc.

Our task is different. We should not europeanize issues, but rather fight for the preservation of basic civil, political and economic liberties.

We need an institutional framework which makes them possible. We need unregulated markets, we need states to guarantee and safeguard the rule of law. The alternative is a non-state, post-democracy and administered society.

We need a New Europe, a Europe without Europeanism. Let us move to a Europe of economic freedom, to Europe of small and non-expanding government, to a Europe without state paternalism, to a Europe without pseudo-moralizing political correctness, to a Europe without intellectual snobbism and elitism, to a Europe without supranational, all-continental ambitions. If somebody across the ocean labels this kind of Europe by the expression "New Europe," it would only be good. However, I must emphasize that we are still very far from it.

The Czech Republic and the EU: A Marriage of Convenience, Not of Love

Speech for The Commonwealth Club of California and World Affairs Council of Northern California, San Francisco, November 8, 2004

When I was last here in San Francisco, six years ago, my country was still in the first decade of its post-communist era. We were still deeply involved in our so-called transformation process. It is not surprising, therefore, that the title of the speech I delivered here then was "The Political Economy of Transition: The Czech Lesson." I discussed the basic structure of this unique historical maneuver — of the move from communism to a free society. I tried to describe the crucial pillars of the whole process — liberalization and deregulation of the administered economy, privatization of a fully state-owned economy, restrictive macroeconomic policy (after decades of repressed inflation), the building of democracy and a market-friendly institutional infrastructure, as well as our attempts to organize this maneuver in a way which would minimize the inevitable transformation costs connected with such a deep and radical systemic change. I also stressed that the transition was done in the real world, not in a laboratory controlled by an omnipotent philosopher-king, by an enlightened president or prime minister.

I tried to explain that "I do not believe in the possibility of a smooth and stable transition in the politically and socially difficult, but highly democratic, pluralistic and open societies (and economies) of Central and Eastern Europe. We are not in a brave new world of perfect markets and perfect government." I do not see any need now to put it differently, even if there are permanent dreams about organizing the transition as a controlled experiment in applied economics.

The transition is over. The Czech Republic has become — structurally — a standard, normal European country and as a result of this it has typical European problems. They cannot be solved by means of another revolution, because we are already in the middle of the process of a spontaneous evolution. This evolutionary era is less radical, less dramatic, less headlines-creating, but — paradoxically — more controversial and even more ideological. This era is also connected with the ongoing European integration process and with our entry into the EU on May 1, 2004. Let me say a few words about it.

Our entry into the EU has been planned and prepared for a long time. Already in November 1989, hundreds of thousands of us — almost subconsciously and thus completely spontaneously — came up with the slogan "Back to Europe" — a slogan that, in its simplicity, became one of the most important symbols of that historic occasion and of our further development. By using this slogan, we wanted to indicate that we intend:

- to overcome the isolation of our country that lasted almost half a century;
- to overcome our unnatural and one-sided orientation towards the East;
- to end our disrespect for the basic values of the political, economic and social systems functioning successfully West of us,
- to end our non-involvement in the activities of those European institutions that had been founded during our absence from the democratic developments of the free part of the European continent between February 1948 and November 1989 and that shaped the face of today's Europe.

I can assure you that this powerful slogan did not suggest any kind of anti-Americanism, as it could be interpreted now. We just wanted to be a free, normally-functioning, prosperous country. "Back to Europe" is, of course, a different slogan than "Avanti into the European Union." Whereas the first slogan can promise benefits, the second one has both costs and benefits. The first journey was straightforward, the second one is more complicated.

On the other hand, the problems are natural. As is common in the lives of individuals as well as in society as a whole, we have gained something by becoming an EU member but at the same time there is something we have lost. One never gets anything for free; as the well-known saying goes there are no free lunches. It is our obligation to do everything to make sure the proportion of gains and losses is favorable, which certainly is not and will not be automatic. We must learn how to remain ourselves, not only as individuals, but as a Czech nation which is more than the sum of individuals and of individual interests. These wider interests do exist and they should not be labelled as nationalism. We are obliged to our predecessors to preserve Czech statehood. The Americans understand patriotism well, much more than contemporary Europeans who consider it as something politically incorrect.

Looking at the European integration process from the broader, not only Czech perspective, the year 2004 will be remembered for two important events in Europe: for — until now — the biggest EU enlargement and for the birth of the EU constitution, which represents a radical step on the way to a — at least nominally — unified Europe and to the gradual disappearance of national states on the European continent.

When we speak about enlargement, there is no doubt that the new members, Central and East European countries, gained important political recognition, that their membership in the EU means an end of the post-communist transformation, as well as an end of the Cold War division of Europe. This is very important. These effects are, however, more symbolic than real.

The real problem is different. The new member countries — as economically less developed countries — need catching-up. They need real convergence. The question is whether the nominal convergence, the acceptance of EU legislation, standards, rules and policies, will accelerate the expected real convergence or block it? The historical evidence is in this respect — at least — mixed. The results depend very much on the existence or non-existence of huge financial transfers because — without them — the nominal convergence creates costs that are higher than the benefits. This problem should be taken seriously because, otherwise, we will be confronted with a huge disappointment of citizens in the new member countries. The case of East Germany is well known, as well as the case of Mezzogiorno in Southern Italy.

Enlargement means a bigger EU and, as a result, the transaction costs of EU functioning will go up. On one hand, the task of governing a bigger and more diversified entity will be more complicated. I am referring to the costs of collecting, using and evaluating the necessary information, the costs of making decisions in a multidimensional, very complicated structure, the costs of implementing and controlling decisions, etc. When we increase the number of countries, while keeping the scope of policies constant, the task of governing will be either more costly or less efficient and/or less democratic. To escape such an unpleasant arithmetic is not possible. At the same time, there will be non-zero costs for individual EU countries connected with their obligatory application of uniform EU decisions and standards.

All of this is amplified by the appearance of the EU constitution, which is a radical document with huge implications for efficiency, democracy and national sovereignty. It aims at eliminating the legal autonomy of individual European countries, it introduces an EU legal personality and, in terms of international law, it transforms the EU into a state.

It can bring about some increase in the operational efficiency of governing, but at the price of:

- the strengthening of the democratic deficit;
- the shift in decision-making procedures – less of a democratic type, more of a hierarchical type;
- more majority voting than unanimity;
- the further depersonification of the EU and the growth of anonymity in decision-making;
- the growing loss of national sovereignty;
- the increasing power of the EU "core," etc.

These unpleasant phenomena cannot be changed by the hypothetically good intentions of EU politicians and bureaucrats. It is a systemic issue.

We should not rely on the god-like characteristics of EU politicians and bureaucrats. We should take a different route. We should not europeanize issues but fight for the preservation of basic civil, political and economic liberties, as well as for a minimal state. We need an institutional framework which makes it possible. We need unregulated markets, we need states to guarantee and safeguard the rule of law. We should know that the alternative is a non-state, post-democracy and administered society.

We need a New Europe, a Europe without Europeanism. We need a Europe of economic freedom, a Europe of small and non-expanding government, a Europe without state paternalism, a Europe without pseudo-moralizing political correctness, a Europe without intellectual snobbism and elitism, a Europe without supranational, continent-wide ambitions. If somebody across the ocean labels this kind of Europe by the expression "New Europe," it would only be good. However, I must emphasize that we are very far from it.

Footnotes to Chapter III

[1] Robert Mundell, "A Theory of Optimum Currency Areas," *American Economic Review*, Vol. 41, No. 3, 1961.

[2] Patrick Bolton, et al., "Economic Theories of the Break-Up and Integration of Nations," Brussels, ECARE, September 1995.

[3] "Rome or Brussels?" Institute of Economic Affairs.

[4] Romano Prodi, interview with Richard Quest, CNN, January 1, 2002.

[5] Quoted in Peter Norman, Lionel Barber and James Blitz, "All the President's Men; Romano Prodi aims to lead a strong EU team," *The Financial Times,* April 9,1999.

[6] Ibid., pp. 29-32 and 36.

[7] Robert Mundell, "A Theory of Optimum Currency Areas."

[8] J. J. Heckman, "Flexibility, Job Creation and Economic Performance," paper presented at the Munich Economic Summit, May 2, 2003, p. 16.

[9] Anthony Coughlan, "Some Reasons Why Joining the Euro Has Been a Mistake for the Republic of Ireland," *European Journal*, Vol. 10, No. 8, July 2003, p. 16.

[10] Herbert Grubel, "New Criteria for Optimum Currency Areas," paper presented at the University of Melbourne, January 23, 2003.

[11] Robert McTeer, "A Skeptical Texan Wishes the Swooning Euro Well," *European Affairs*, Vol. 1, No. 2, Spring 2002.

[12] Anthony Coughlan, "Some Reasons Why Joining the Euro Has Been a Mistake for the Republic of Ireland," p. 16.

[13] Anthony de Jasay, "Free-Riding on the Euro," *Library of Economics and Liberty*, September 17, 2003, p. 2.

[14] Peter B. Kenen, "Sorting Out Some EMU Issues," Reprint No. 29, December 1996, Princeton University.

[15] Hans Eichel, *Sunday Times*, December 23, 2001.

[16] H. W. Sinn and F. Westermann, "Two Mezzogiornos," CESIFO Working Paper Series, No. 378, 2001.

Václav Klaus on Inauguration Day, Prague, Czech Republic, March 7, 2003.

Chapter IV:

REFLECTIONS ON THE WORLD

The Czech Republic and a Secure Europe

Speech at the Center for Strategic and International Studies Statesmen's Forum, September 30, 1996, Washington D.C.

I am a little bit hesitant to talk to this distinguished audience and to make the strong statements about strategic issues which you all expect from me here.

One has to start with making one's implicit assumptions explicit. I am always puzzled whenever I hear self-assured statements about fundamental global strategic issues without explicit analysis of the behavior of individual players of the game, or statements based on false assumptions, on obsolete ideas of the world. Therefore, instead of making strong statements about Russia, China, Bosnia, etc., I wish to give a few comments on my interpretation of the post-Cold War world. The conclusions should be drawn by someone else.

The postcommunist and post-Cold War era demonstrates a visible movement forward. To interpret it differently means to be disappointed with what has happened since 1989. For me, we are moving, we are on the road to a better world, to a world without totalitarian regimes (at least when we talk about Europe and America, about our common Atlantic region), without threatening military structures, without totally inefficient economic systems, without over-ideologized thinking. We have not yet entered heaven and we will never make it, but I am confident that we are on the right track. I know there are people among us who see crisis in any moment when there is no central authority in full control of all events, when there is no *dirigisme* from above, when we witness more spontaneity in human behavior than somebody's intentions, whenever there is anything new, unknown, unplanned and unprepared, when the old clichés are lost or forgotten. I do not belong to that group.

We have probably entered a new period, but I see it as a chance, not as a problem.

I know, of course, that human society is very fragile (and vulnerable to all kinds of disturbances), and to think that we will be able to move forward without a permanent effort, without daily involvement of all of us in a never-ending fight for freedom, would be a fatal mistake, a "fatal conceit," and would take us on "the road to serfdom," which some of us know too well. To think that the collapse of communism and its probable definitive end is a final victory, the "end of history," would be very costly. We all see new dangers around us, new blind alleys, new attempts to create "brave new worlds" based on very promising rhetoric, on more sincere or less sincere intentions but on wrong ambitions and false assumptions about human behavior.

The idea of transatlantic cooperation between Europe and North America was born at the end of World War II. The tragic experience of our fathers and grandfathers with fascist dictatorships, with communism and with the devastating war, and their resolution not to go through it again led to many postwar activities and to the formation of several international organizations, especially NATO.

The transatlantic cooperation was for decades kept together by an imminent communist threat and we subconsciously accepted the idea that NATO was an anticommunist bloc and nothing else. With the end of communism, the common enemy disappeared and some of us seem to be at a loss what to fight for.

I am not. For me, the transatlantic community was never connected solely with one past enemy. It has deeper roots and a stronger basis. It is based *on ideas, not on enemies*. It is connected with the tradition of freedom, democracy and the market economy. Liberalism (in its original, European meaning) represents our common cultural heritage which we try to keep alive for future generations on both sides of the Atlantic Ocean. We are committed to such a duty and we have to guard it in all spheres, including the security one.

I am aware of existing dangers and know that for the time being they are more in the field of ideas than in the field of security. Some of them are "domestic" and are connected with new attempts at the corporativization and syndicalization of our societies, with attempts to legislatively support organizations and associations, partializing us, filling the space between individuals and the state at the expense of both and denying the elementary principles of a liberal society. Such approaches are justified — erroneously — by well-intentioned people who, instead of advocating further "de-statization" through liberalization, deregulation and privatization (not just in the economic sphere), advocate not freedom but new versions of collectivism, not overall healthy competition but more and more areas controlled by experts, professionals and "better" people, not the acceptance of incrementalism and improvements of Pareto optimality but isolated, absolutist "solutions" to partial problems, not a coherent society but new "feudalities" (to use Ludwig Erhard's term), etc.

Such tendencies, when winning at home, will have enormous influence upon international relations, upon transatlantic cooperation, and we should not underestimate them. Our foreign policy reactions and initiatives are less autonomous than it is often assumed, and their roots in domestic ideological tenets are very deep.

I see the danger of the increase of *isolationist* tendencies in both Europe and America, even if it is for different reasons. In Europe it is because of more deepening than widening in the integration philosophy, because of less vigorous market forces and less vigorous individualist traditions. In America it is because of the prevalence of new, less liberal ideologies and because of traditional self-centeredness in world affairs. I see external dangers as well, but I consider them less dangerous than our own deficiencies.

For several decades, we in my country lived in a closed society. We know what it means to stress differences and hatred instead of searching for commonalities and friendship. I believe the original postwar transatlantic idea arose as a reaction to our prewar closeness and we should not repeat our mistakes. The disappearance of one common enemy should not demotivate us. We know that the slippery road to serfdom is not very far away and that some parts of the road may offer seductive views of the natural beauties around.

Churchill and NATO Enlargement to the East

Speech at the Churchill Symposium 1997, Zurich, Switzerland, September 18, 1997

Fifty-one years ago, one year after the War, at a moment of growing tension between free societies and the dangerous Soviet communist imperium, this city and this university prepared a perfect opportunity for an unforgettable speech by one of the most prophetic European politicians of that time, Sir Winston Churchill. As we know now, he used this opportunity to express several important ideas which influenced the shape of the world, and especially of Europe, for the whole remaining part of this century.[1]

Now, at the end of this century and looking into the next one, we are at another decisive postwar moment, even if the war in the last 50 years was more or less "only" a cold one. Nevertheless, after the end of communism the world has changed and we need new visions and — as a consequence of them — new bold initiatives. I stress visions and ideas because it has been proved many times that ideas have consequences. We need another Winston Churchill and another Zürich speech. My modest remarks today are definitely without any ambition in this respect. I will try to make just a few comments using my very specific perspective — being prime minister of a postcommunist country located in the heart of Europe — to add something to the ongoing debate.

I would like, first, to present some arguments in favor of the continuation of NATO's existence, second, to advocate the enlargement of NATO to the East and finally, to express my deep conviction that this development will help stabilize Europe and will enhance its coherence and integrity — on condition, of course, that Europe itself will not make wrong moves in other fields.

1. To be able to do this, we have to put the meaning and role of NATO into a broader historical and geopolitical perspective. To believe that the collapse of communism and its probable definitive end is a final victory, the "end of history," as some suggest, would be very costly. I see around us new dangers, new blind alleys, new threats, new conflicts, new attempts to create "brave new worlds" based on wrong ambitions and false assumptions as in any moment in the past. I hope that we all are aware of those new dangers and that we all know as well that in the globalized world of today, geographical distance does not have that much importance. There is no doubt that we need international cooperation and — as Winston Churchill stressed so strongly — that we need

transatlantic cooperation, that we need an American presence in Europe. We need it in many fields, but in both the spiritual and security fields more than in any other ones.

The idea of transatlantic cooperation between Europe and North America was born at the end of World War II. The tragic experience of our fathers and grandfathers with fascist dictatorships, with communism and with the devastating world war, as well as their resolution not to go through the same development again, led to many postwar activities and to the formation of several important international organizations, including NATO. The Czechs (and Slovaks) were among the founding fathers of the UN, IMF, World Bank and GATT, but the Iron Curtain did not allow us to be present at the birth of NATO. And we regretted it deeply and we paid for it dearly.

Transatlantic cooperation was — for decades past — maintained by an imminent communist threat and many of us, consciously or subconsciously, accepted the notion that NATO is an anticommunist bloc and nothing else. With the end of communism the visible and tangible enemy disappeared and some of us seemed to be at a loss what to fight for. I do not have such a problem.

For me (and I am convinced that not only for me), the transatlantic community was never connected solely with one past enemy. It had deeper roots and a stronger basis. If we look at Churchill's speech today, we can see that he stressed the Christian faith, Christian ethics, that he stressed culture, arts, philosophy and science. For me and for him, the transatlantic community was and is based *on ideas, not on enemies*. It is connected with the European and American tradition of freedom, democracy and the market economy. This tradition is based on our common cultural and civilization heritage which — I suppose — we are obliged to keep alive for future generations on both sides of the Atlantic Ocean. John O'Sullivan, editor of *National Review* and founder of the New Atlantic Initiative, recently put it in a similar way: "The alliance is the military expression of Western civilization — in fact the only institution that encompasses all the West." I strongly believe that exactly for that reason we all need NATO now, and we will need it in the future as well.

2. What about the enlargement of NATO? There is no doubt that the three invited countries, and, undoubtedly, some other European countries, belong to the same community of nations. I know that the invitation issued for three Central European countries to join NATO, and announced at the recent Madrid

summit, created new questions, if not tensions, both inside and outside NATO, both among noninvited countries and among the opponents of enlargement. It is not my aspiration to discuss the criteria used for the selection of the three chosen countries because I am supposed to be biased in this respect. Nevertheless, I would like to say that I would always accept that the decision of one or another prestigious Zürich tennis club to offer me a membership is, and should be, its own decision, not mine. However, taking into account the degree of systemic transformation and the rapid progress in establishing free society, based on a pluralistic parliamentary democracy and on a market economy, achieved in the three invited countries, I would dare to argue that the choice was rational and "just."

It is evident that the enlargement of NATO has non-zero costs for all participants and that there must not be any free-riding. I can assure you that we are aware of it and are prepared to bear the necessary costs. I believe that NATO's members are ready to cover their part of the costs of enlargement as well, but it seems to me that this is something which must be explicitly stated. The ratification process will give us very important information in this respect.

3. Speaking about Europe, we have to discuss the question of how NATO enlargement is connected with the current European institutional restructuring, with the strong European unionistic ambitions which are characteristic for the '90s. I believe, and now I quote from the Churchill speech: ". . .hundreds of millions of people want to be happy and free, prosperous and safe." We all want such a Europe and we consider European integration to be one of the instruments for achieving these goals.

The distinction between instruments and goals is for me always — and in the rather fuzzy debate about Europe even more — absolutely crucial. It is frustrating to see this difference blurred so often. European integration (and its potential variants) should not become a goal in itself or a substitute for other goals. I am, however, afraid that this is the way it has been approached in many European debates in the last decade.

It seems quite obvious to me that the form European integration takes should depend on the goals themselves, on their ranking, on the relative weights given to them as well as on the existing tradeoffs among them.

Is there an additive quality, or perhaps an incompatibility, or a tradeoff between freedom and peace, between peace and prosperity, or between freedom and prosperity? The answer is not self-evident. I have the feeling that current European unification ambitions (including the European Monetary Union) stem from the assumption that some of the goals are superior to some other goals. To put it clearly, the insufficiently structured and specified goal called peace (or security or safety or the reduction of the risk of another intra-European war among individual nation-states) has for some of us such a special position that it almost blocks any serious debate about other goals or about existing tradeoffs. It has been sometimes even used as a "dummy" for some hidden goals, which I am convinced is something we have to avoid.

I guess Winston Churchill would put it in a similar way. He would probably address the issues straight on. He would look back and remind us of the World War II experience with the hope that we can learn something. His phrase in his Zürich speech: "Is it the only lesson of history that mankind is unteachable?" is in this respect very explicit. He would try to define priorities and the sequencing or ordering of existing goals.

For me, and in this respect, I am undoubtedly biased by my personal experience with life in a communist regime, and convinced that absolute priority should be placed upon freedom — I mean upon the specific relationship between an individual and the state. My oversensitivity in seeing or sensing various open or hidden forms of the suppression of freedom is notorious. It tells me that we should do our best to stop the continuously repeating tendencies towards excessive regulation of human activities, towards unproductive government intervention at the micro level, towards various forms of quasi-generous paternalism, of dangerous elitism, of ambitious social engineering. We have to be on guard and that is the main reason why the extremely fruitful transatlantic relationship should continue and why the role of NATO in Europe and for Europe will be as important in the future as it was in the past.

This is the core of the message I wanted to share with you today. To repeat, I believe that NATO is here to stay, that NATO enlargement will reinforce NATO itself, and that the stability of Europe will be strengthened as well. The future, therefore, has a good chance.

Society and the Crisis of Liberalism, or Liberalism as a Hope for Society?

Alpbach Forum Seminar on "Society and the Crisis of Liberalism," August 22, 1998

It is always fashionable to talk about a crisis. It gives those who use such terminology a special aura that they see the world more sharply than the rest of us, that they possess a noble vision of a better world, and that they know how to get there. The question is where the feeling or certainty of a crisis starts — in a deep and penetrating analysis of the status quo or in an aprioristic, elitist and moralistic ambition? Is it merely a new fashion in thinking, an attempt to create a niché in the very competitive market of ideas or is it a real breakthrough?

At the very beginning of my talk today, I must confess that I do not see any crisis around me, that I do not see any *zerrissene Gesellschaft* mentioned in the title of this seminar, that I do not know any feasible alternative to Western liberalism, and especially that I do not believe in authoritarian, constructivistic ways to create a "brave new world" (of any form, color or smell). My position is based both on theoretical arguments in economics and other social sciences and on my personal experience with communism and its transformation into a free, open society — which we have had an opportunity to experience in the last decade. Both sources of arguments have the same importance to me.

No one would dare to claim that we are approaching paradise. There are many problems in the real world and no one should neglect or underestimate them. The only issue is how to tackle them, what to do with them. Some of us believe in individual human beings and in their motivation to better the world around them, provided basic institutions of society make it possible. Some believe in themselves and in the government which could realize their recommendations about what to do with the world they have ambitions to bring to perfection. We should agree with Thomas Sowell that these two approaches very clearly describe the current "Conflict of Visions" and that the second, antiliberal vision is "The Vision of the Anointed" (to make use of the titles of his two important books).

I strongly believe in the liberal world order. Such a world is, of course, not without preconditions. Together with Margaret Thatcher, I am convinced that "the life of free men and women has to be a life of self-discipline, self-control and self-sacrifice," and in this respect it has to be based on an elementary moral system. At the same time, I believe in the inherent morality of markets, in the ethics of work and saving, in the crucial link between freedom and private property. It is not possible (or desirable) to legislate a better world from above or outside.

Such a way of thinking has been recently put under a new, strong and dangerous attack. The adjective "dangerous" is appropriate because I see a virus of demagogy and romanticism in the visions of the preachers of communitarianism, or a civic society as it is called in some countries. There is no identity between the two terms, but the idea of civic society (in its current, Central European meaning) has many similarities with communitarianism. And I am aware of the dangers of this idea. There was perhaps some justification of (or an excuse for) the idea of a civic society in the communist era, when it was one of the strategies for resistance (though I never shared this strategy). Communism is over, but the old antiliberal ideas are still with us. They can be seen in continuous attempts to find third ways, to integrate markets with nonmarkets, to construct capitalism with a human face, to attack individualism (by caricaturing it), to mix genuine, spontaneously evolving associations of individuals with organizations based on obligatory membership, to disregard the crucial role of private property, etc.

Communitarianism, as I see it, represents a new version of an old antiliberal approach to society, a shift from traditional liberal democracy to new forms of collectivism, a romantic dream and "a constructivistic attempt at imposing the moral system of the face-to-face group on the large, anonymous society," a new way of integrating society by organizing it at a micro level.[2] (Communitarianism may, however, also be a simple and much more modest empirical hypothesis that a deeper and denser network of human associations creates more social capital, but real communitarianism is much more.)

My first argument regards the communitarian analysis of contemporary society. They interpret it as an *egoistic, individualistic world*, where the basic form of social interaction takes place among atomistic units (human beings). They are supposedly alone, which means not rooted in various social institutions which would give them anything other than purely egoistic motives for behavior. I disagree with such an interpretation of events. I do not think it reflects the prevailing atmosphere in our society. It may describe a more or less pathological situation of some individuals with problems of association, but not the real world we know and live in.

There is — with all known undermining and weakening factors and influences — *the family*, which remains the main foundation of our society and of our public life. In addition to the family, we are — mostly voluntarily — *members of other social institutions,* which brings us into contact with other people. It starts with schools, with the places where we work, with free time activities (such as sports clubs), etc. The more active we are, the more people we meet and collaborate with. To caricature life in the contemporary Western world as an uncooperative game (or fight) of isolated, self-centered and self-interested individuals is not justified. We should not be ashamed of self-interest because it is not true that self-interest is a motivation unworthy of human beings. In addition, we know — at least since Adam Smith — that society cannot rest on the noblest motives, and we know as well that self-interest is the strongest motive, whether we like it or not. It does not imply that self-interest blocks our interest in other people and their well-being. In the language of economics, we can say that the well-being of other people can be, and very often is, a factor in our "utility function" (with a positive sign).

My second argument relates to communitariansm as an alternative ideology. I have already mentioned some of my arguments, but I would like to repeat the two most important ones:

- communitarianism wants *to change human beings* (instead of taking them as they are);
- communitarianism in its aversion to individualism and its advocacy of coercive ways of human association is *another form of collectivism.*

We are — with our communist past — oversensitive to both aspects of communitarianism.

Because of ambitions to change human beings, communitarianism is *a form of elitism.* Its advocates have the feeling that they have been chosen to advise, to moralize, to know better than the "normal" people what is right or wrong, what the people should do, what will be good for them. They want us not only to be free, but to be good, just and moral as well — using, of course, their definition of what good, just and moral is. Like Margaret Thatcher, I start with the assumption that liberty is an individual quality and, therefore, we should not collectivize it.

Communitarianism wants to *socialize us* by forcing us into artificial, not genuine, not spontaneously formed groups or groupings. In this respect, it is another version of corporativism or syndicalism, of organizations with obligatory membership which bring together people of the same profession, age, habits or interests. We used to live in a "world of obligatory memberships." There was one tourist organization, one organization of pet fans, one horse-riding club etc. And we know what it means. For that reason, we want to be "free to choose" (or eventually not to choose).

My third argument regards *how to get to the brave new world of communitarianism.* One dangerous procedure for getting there is to create an intellectual climate hostile to traditional Western liberalism. This proved to be very easy to do and very efficient. After the collapse of communism, in the moment of a strange, ideological vacuum, communitarianism (and environmentalism) took their chance. They came with new arguments against our contemporary society, relied on the feeling of "the end of ideologies" and based their tactics on people´s inclination to permanently search for something new (or quasi-new).

Communitarianism cannot win through preaching only. Its preachers are here, but they cannot start a mass movement which would lead to a social revolution. Instead, they try to reach the legislators and *legislate the world according to their dreams.* And this is something I am afraid of, because we live in a world of "unconstrained" parliamentarianism. When I say unconstrained, I mean unconstrained by the feeling of the whole of society and of its fragility. Milton Friedman recently put it crystal clear: "We are ruled by a majority, but it is a majority composed of a coalition of minorities.... No minority has any incentive to be concerned about the cumulative effects of the measures passed."[3] And this is very dangerous, especially when the decision-makers' and legislators' thinking is based on "an incredible mishmash of pseudosocial science, pop psychology, vacuous moralizing, rank ideology, and political bias."[4] It is our task to limit the introduction of systemic changes based on such aprioristic backgrounds and motivations, and instead to rely on spontaneous evolution of human institutions.

If the communitarians concentrated on founding specific institutions and on working in them, I would be on their side. But it must be done retail, not wholesale. It is necessary to do something specific, not to keep advising others what to do.

Liberty and the Rule of Law

Lecture, "Leadership for America," The Heritage Foundation, Philadelphia, April 22, 1999

It is a great honor to be invited to deliver the 1999 "Leadership for America" lecture for the Heritage Foundation. It is an additional honor to do it in Philadelphia (the city we need so much these days in Europe, where we see a steady accretion of power to central regulatory authorities in Brussels without anything like the original American Constitution, which specified the areas of competence for federal government and left the rest to the states). And finally, it is an honor to be asked to talk about "Liberty and the Rule of Law" for someone who comes from Central Europe and spent most of his life in an oppressive communist regime where there was neither liberty nor rule of law.

I do not want to pretend that I know more about liberty than you or that I have a comparative advantage in discussing it, but I would dare to argue that I know more about the absence of liberty, and especially about the tragic consequences of its absence. Because of my personal experience, I do not take liberty for granted. I know as well that, looking at human history, its existence is an exception, not the rule, and for that reason I may be oversensitive to the first signals of its distortions and all kinds of replacements (by something else, to put it mildly). I am also sufficiently aware of its fragility and nonpermanence.

The decade of the '90s started with many hopes connected mostly with the collapse of communism and with the end of the Cold War. It was at the same time the moment of "takeoff" in many developing countries. In addition, it coincided with the victory of Reaganite–Thatcherite policies in many developed countries. Liberty and free markets were on the winning side, and both "hard" and "soft" variants of socialism (or communism) were visibly in retreat.

At the end of the '90s the mood is quite different. The expectations-reality gap in transition countries is growing (and not closing). In spite of many positive achievements in most of the countries (which may be empirically documented), the expectations have grown much faster. The communist era has become more or less forgotten and everyone already wants to enjoy all the advantages of living in a mature and rich capitalist society and economy without taking into consideration the past, relatively slow evolutionary process in human society, and especially the unavoidable tradeoffs.

Emerging, developing markets in Asia, Latin America or Africa — after several successful years — surprisingly and unexpectedly fell into a new, dangerous reform trap. Rapid growth was replaced by stagnation, excess demand by excess supply, inflow of capital by its outflow, the belief in free markets by belief in government intervention, optimism by pessimism.

The developed countries in Europe and North America have suddenly become dominated by socialist governments, by new methods of and arguments for government intervention, by myriad regulations, controls and prohibitions, by fashionable speculations about "Third Ways," by fantasies about liberalism (in the European meaning of that term) "with a human face," by seductive slogans of communitarianism, by the fallacies of environmentalism, etc.

Liberty and free markets are faced with insidious threats as before or, perhaps, more than before. This is, of course, not the slightest reason for giving up, for not continuing our never-ending struggle for liberty and responsibility, for liberty and its accompanying preconditions — which include the general moral order on the one hand and the rule of law on the other.

I would like now — instead of preaching about the ideas and values most of us share — to make a few comments concerning some of the causes of the situation that now exists at the turn of the century. Their selection undoubtedly reflects my perspective, my experience and the limits of my intellectual horizons.

1. It is no understatement to say that *the defense of liberty and free markets is out of fashion*. Influential intellectuals have written and published their important books and they already occupied all the niches in the complicated and very oligopolistic market of ideas. The demand for new products of the old variety is declining and the law of diminishing returns is very powerful in the field of ideas as in any other human activity. The profession of "scribes" moved to another topic. We should not forget that and should increase our own activities.

2. After several decades of analyzing and criticizing *the enormous government failure* which was more visible and tangible in Soviet-type economies than in other parts of the world, the socialists of all types returned to the concept of *market failure* and, equipped with very sophisticated economic techniques and instruments, they succeeded in changing the prevailing atmosphere. They have got new arguments by seeing the current complications of various emerging markets where weak, shallow and therefore not fully efficient markets, released from the old bondages by radical liberalization, deregulation and privatization, do not demonstrate the same results as markets created by long, uninterrupted

spontaneous evolution. They should — together with all of us — welcome and support the ongoing changes, but they — with their high-brow, arrogant approach — prefer to dismiss them as "an experiment in instant capitalism." Such simplifications and misinterpretations of history should be refuted. It is, however, quite often accepted together with an ahistoric criticism of imperfect markets, societies, laws and constitutions.

I was recently struck while reading an article written by one of the gurus of the new *etatist* approach, Joseph Stiglitz (who as vice president of the World Bank has enormous influence), that he sees "the philosophies of the 1970s and 1980s as a fallacy" because "the central role that government played in planning and programming was seen as part of the problem of development rather than as part of the solution."[5] I am afraid our response to it is not sufficient and is not loud and self-confident enough.

3. In addition to the traditional antimarket attacks on freedom and liberty, we are facing the emergence of two new powerful ideologies which are gradually gaining ground — *environmentalism* on the one hand and *communitarianism* on the other. I consider both of them to be great problems.

4. I can say with some simplification that until now I have been talking about the role of ideas. It is, however, necessary to talk about the power of vested interests as well, and especially about its recent relative increase in importance. We see the new and increasing role of coalitions of interest groups, which plague the legislature with sectional (very partial) demands, and we see dispersed voters who have little rational incentive to organize themselves to control them. As Norman Barry put it recently: "well-organized and committed minorities always have an interest in formulating policies that are inconsistent with the long-run aims and purposes of an apathetic and rationally ignorant populace."[6] It means that "more democracy," which by the way brings about another version of the "soft state," is not an answer to the rent-seeking behavior.

It is very easy to talk about law and the rule of law. But we should talk more about problems connected with the formation of legislation — in transition economies, in emerging markets, in developed democracies — than about legislation as such. There have always been vested interests, but their role now is probably greater than before — even if we can quote Adam Smith or John Stuart Mill discussing them. In my part of the world, the collapse of communism led to the disappearance of all past rent-seeking groups and it took

— fully in accordance with Mancur Olson's hypothesis — some time to form and organize them again. But I have to say that they are there again — in less than a decade.

We see the absence of the rule of law in some parts of the world, but we should not criticize it on moralistic grounds. It should be interpreted with the help of cost/benefit analysis of human behavior. Talking about liberty, I am no less afraid of the misuse of the rule of law. Because of the role of vested interests and their relative success in influencing legislation, the law becomes in many fields oppressive itself. I consider as extremely significant the growing role of regulative or administrative legislation, or to put it differently, the growing role of the legislation of vertical relations as compared to the legislation of horizontal relations. This is the result of the feeling of inadequacy of horizontal relations and of the growing belief in the importance of vertical relations. We have to challenge it. There is on the one hand the "sacredness" of the legislation and on the other the "dubiety" (or problematicality) of its formation. There is no perfect system of law (which could hypothetically exist only in a vacuum, in a world without human beings). We should aim at a Pareto-optimal system, which is the result of the real world and of genuine human interests and their relative power.

All of that is important generally, but even more so for the appropriate interpretation of the problems of transition. We are rapidly rebuilding our legislation (but we know that the system of law is a Hayekian complex system which is based on evolution, not construction) and we are heavily criticized for not having created a perfect system. It is more complicated than our critics assume.

To conclude, there is no need for pessimism. But there is no room for passivity and inactivity. We have to continue our endless fight for liberty and the rule of law and I am sure we will do it.

The Third Way and Its Fatal Conceits

Speech at the Mont Pelerin Society Regional Meeting, Vancouver, Canada, August 30, 1999

When, several months ago, I received a letter from Milton Friedman inviting me to say a few words here about the "Third Way," I answered positively, without the slightest hesitation. All my life I have been trying to resist anything resembling a Third Way between socialism and freedom and because of it, it seemed to me that it would be easy to talk about it.

When I started to prepare my manuscript and to search for hard arguments, persuasive quotations and relevant literature and when I began to structure my thoughts, I discovered that the topic is not well-defined, that there are almost no serious academic contributions to such a discussion, and that we can find either crude, usually almost empty political statements or journalistic, very superficial articles but nothing in between.

I am afraid I will not be able to make any substantial breakthrough today. I can only add some arguments to the discussion by looking at the chosen problem from the viewpoint of someone who had been openly rejecting the idea of a Third Way already while living in a communist society and in the process of its dismantling. In this respect, I am here in a minority.

After the fall of communism, almost 10 years ago, during one of my first opportunities to address a Western audience, I was applauded at the World Economic Forum in Davos for saying: "The Third Way is the fastest way to the third world." It seemed to me at that time that Third Way thinking was so discredited — together with communism — that no one would dare to defend it or to push forward with it again.

I was wrong. The collapse of communism created a strange vacuum which was very rapidly filled with one, always available ideology — the ideology of those who disliked liberalism (in the Mont Pelerin Society sense), who did not believe in freedom and free markets, who believed more in themselves and in their own privileged role and position in society, who considered themselves enlightened and "anointed" (as the word is used by Thomas Sowell in his well-known book), progressive and better than the rest of us. They were clever to call their own ideology at that time "the end of ideologies." The adherents of those views looked for an alternative name and some of them started to call it the "Third Way." There is, probably, nothing more and nothing less to it.

The disillusion with communism on the one hand and the popularity of Margaret Thatcher's and Ronald Reagan's policies on the other made it impossible to openly advocate obsolete socialist dreams, fallacies and old-fashioned remedies for current economic and social problems. It was necessary to come up with a new product or, what is usually better and easier, with *an old product in new packaging*. In this respect, *the Third Way of the 1990s is just a new attempt to save socialism, social democratism and the welfare state.* As we know, there are only two "ways" in human society and some of us are convinced — and I belong to that group — that the so-called Third Way is a euphemistic and dangerously misleading name for the second way — socialism.

Tony Blair recently made a very apt statement: "The Third Way is a new alliance between progress and justice."[7] I know that it is difficult or almost impossible for us to take such a statement seriously, but we should have. It was a mistake that such a formula was not immediately analyzed and attacked — we either did not care or were not able to easily discuss such fuzzy words like alliance, progress and justice and especially their unspecified combination. We can laugh at it but we must be aware of the fact that such loose phrases have been more or less accepted as a new basic dogma, as a currently dominant antiliberal ideology.

For the adherents of the Mont Pelerin Society way of thinking, there is nothing new in this new version of "Third Wayism" and all our old arguments against socialism, corporativism, technocratism, social engineering, elitism, *etatism*, interventionism, etc., are relevant again. The advocates of Third Way thinking, however, do not listen. Therefore, we have to be more specific and more explicit. The target is fuzzy and moving. The Third Wayism is not a closed group of people, not a well-defined political structure, and not a clear philosophy or ideology. The term "Third Way" was used in the past by many very different people — by Franco in Spain, by Tito in Yugoslavia, by Swedish social democrats after the war, by Ota Šik in my country at the moment of the Prague Spring era (and we all know that it provoked a Soviet invasion), by Gorbachev at the time of perestroika, by Clinton and his New Democrats, by Blair and his New Labor, by Václav Havel and his fellow travelers in postcommunist countries and by many others. Each one of them tried (and tries now) to be considered a synonym for modernity, progress, wisdom, reason, openness, etc. It is not true.

The Third Way remains a very vague concept which has no operational definition, which has not been properly defined. That blocks its serious discussion but it does not block its use and its irresponsible dissemination, and it does not devalue the promises it contains.

It is not only vague, it is "wide" and expansive as well.

It was originally used in the economic field. Those who did not like both central planning and free markets (and I would add: did not understand both central planning and free markets) preferred to promote Third Ways which — in their naïve understanding — were shaky mixtures of central planning, interventionism and markets. It seems useless to repeat to this audience the arguments of Mises and Hayek which were used in their dispute with Lange, Lerner, Dickinson and other advocates of market socialism in the '30s. It seems superfluous to return to the arguments used against German *Soziale Marktwirtschaft*. It represents another example of a Third Way and we have to admit that its beginning was connected with a famous MPS member, Ludwig Erhard. To be fair, I have to stress that he defined it differently than current German politicians — in both SPD and CDU.[8]

The present-day exponents of Third Way thinking have been relatively successful in pretending that they endorse conservative economic policies — which is, of course, not true. We should not be misled by their rhetoric. They never discuss details, they never reveal what they have in mind when they talk about regulation and they never suggest how to solve the grave financial problems of high levels of government expenditures on their social welfare programs.

The Third Way has its place in political thinking as well, and these days it represents a very fashionable approach to politics and policy-making. It has appeared in many countries, but there cannot be a better example of it than in the apolitical politics of Václav Havel in my country in the whole decade following the collapse of communism. It has been based on a strong disbelief in classical liberal democracy, in political parties, in representative democracy and, on the contrary, on a strong belief in direct democracy, in the leading role of intellectual elites, and in their ability to introduce "a civilization of peace and love" without complications connected with the standard mechanisms so typical for the 20th century "age of politics" which they want to overcome.

The Third Way exists in international politics as well. The bureaucratic, nongenuine, nonspontaneous, nonevolutionary, and therefore artificial unification of Europe, the enormous growth of various international institutions (with dubious competences), the attempts to introduce universal jurisdiction, and NATO's bombing of Yugoslavia are a few examples of the Third Way approach to international politics. What is probably new and definitely dangerous is the fact that current Third Way politicians abandoned the traditional, deep-rooted pacifism of the left and are ready to disseminate their ideas by force if necessary.

Together with the birth of communitariarism (or civic society as it is called in some countries), we have witnessed a Third Way in the moral or cultural field as well. Its advocates propose a new ethical system of thought but do not understand that morality and culture are complex systems which cannot be designed, that they represent a typical example of systems which ought to evolve in the process of human activity, which cannot be created by law, decree or advice. They want to impose their own view of morality and culture upon us whether we want it or not.

What is the origin or source of all that? I am convinced that it is connected with faith in socialism, with the aprioristic disbelief in liberalism and individualism, with inherent collectivism and *etatism*, with the neglect of the tragic experience with the totalitarian systems of the 20th century, with not reading Hayek, with not listening to those who try to warn against the well-known, widely discussed and sufficiently documented ills of this strange century. It is based on constructivistic rationalism, on the pretense of knowledge, on the misunderstanding of limitations of human reason, on the ambitions of the elites. It is based as well on the misuse of humanistic or pseudo-humanistic ideas. In this respect, it is fair to mention another MPS founding father, who also accepted the term "Third Way" — Wilhelm Roepke.[9] But it seems to me that today he would prefer a "free" society to society with all other adjectives, including something which sounds so positive and sympathetic as the adjective "humane."

The Third Way advocates, exponents and propagandists never discuss methods which would have to be used to realize their goals or promises. They do not explicitly describe the substance and logic of the vertical relations in society they propose. And this is their fatal error (or maybe a clever omission). I agree with Kenneth Minogue, who recently said that "any discussion that talks about society and does not deal fully with the state is dishonest."[10] The propagandists of Third Wayism have not suggested new methods of governing and commanding society, new methods of overcoming the problem of the dispersion of knowledge, new methods of solving the Public Choice school arguments concerning the motivation of individuals who represent the government, etc.

Anthony Giddens, a very influential adviser of Tony Blair, in a recent book, *The Third Way: The Renewal of Social Security Democracy,* already in the title puts together Third Way with social democratism.[11] He is at least sincere. His book suggests seven basic reasons for the activity of the government in society he would like to promote:

1. the provision of public goods;
2. the regulation of markets in the public interest;
3. the fostering of social peace;
4. the active development of human capital through a central role by the state in the education system, thereby shaping norms and values;
5. the provision of infrastructure;
6. the fostering of regional and transnational alliances and the pursuit of global goals; and finally,
7. the role of the state as a prime employer in macro- and microeconomic institutions and, especially, in ecological matters.[12]

When we look at the list we have to admit that three items belong to the classical liberal way of thinking but we have to stress that the rest of them would give enormous power to politicians at the expense of individual freedom.

The relevant question in this context is about the future, about the potential inner dynamics of society based on Third Way ideas. Where will it lead Western society if implemented? Will it make a fundamental change as compared to the current state?

It is probably an exaggeration to make a cheap point that the Third Way inevitably leads to serfdom, as some of us were or are inclined to suggest. The socialist and social democratic ideas have been with us for a long time. There is no doubt that they visibly undermined the functioning of the markets and especially the inherent morality of free markets. Will the Third Way suggestions (if implemented) be only a marginal extension of old socialist ideas and not, therefore, fundamentally change contemporary society, or will they bring about a significant change?

I have to admit that I do not expect an important change. The Third Way represents rather a new justification for old socialist ideas and practices than anything else. This is, nevertheless, dangerous. For those of us who are concerned about various "creeping" phenomena and tendencies — where I include the welfare state, expanding government, bureaucratization of society, attempts of various interest groups to better themselves at the expense of others, a hostile and irrational distrust of free markets and their protagonists, etc., whose support fluctuates in time — we must expect that the new wave of "Third Wayism" may complicate our efforts to defend free markets and freedom in general because it may seduce some people who have been our original supporters.

I do not see an imminent danger in the economic field in a narrow sense. I see a much bigger danger of "Third Wayism" in the field of politics (domestically and especially internationally) and I am really afraid of the preachers of new morality and culture. It may come back to the economy, but with a delay.

To conclude, it is our task to fight the Third Way and to expose the pretension of the innocent romanticism of various contemporary gurus of Third Wayism because it is (and they are) not innocent.

How I See This War

Clanek, March 24, 2003

In an extensive interview with *Hospodářské noviny* (on March 21), I was asked what, in my opinion, is the reason behind the current military operation against Iraq. I did not reply, as I knew that an answer couldn't be condensed into one simple sentence. That is why I want to use the format of this article to express my opinions on that topic a little bit more extensively.

War is a terrible thing. This is not a pacifist or a scared phrase from me, but an expression of my fundamental conviction. And not only mine. We live in a country which has a long historical experience with war and the suffering which goes hand in hand with it. Although the youngest generations have, fortunately, not experienced a war directly — I myself remember the War only as a little child — it is obvious that the vast majority of our public realizes quite well what horrors any war brings, both to soldiers and to the civilian population. And (the public realizes) that we must therefore measure, not twice, but 10 times, before we allow generals to take control of resolving political problems and disputes among states.

But that is only one side of the problem. The second one asks: How strong must the motive be for saying that there was no other solution but the military one? In the case of the attack on Iraq, were the reasons humanitarian, ideological, economic, strategic, security, military or some combination of these?

The idea that the Americans are fighting in Iraq because of oil is laughable and naive. The United States is not dependent on Iraqi oil, and if the oil trade needs anything, it is stability and peace in the oil-deposit regions. I therefore think that we must look for reasons elsewhere. *I would look for them in a combination of American idealism, new fears after September 11, and the state of the world after the breakup of the bipolar order, when the United States has become the only real power.* This combination leads to entirely new processes which, however, raise many questions.

There is no question that Iraq was a dictatorship in all its aspects, which is an arrangement unacceptable and potentially dangerous for today's Euro-Atlantic civilization. But the idea of the proponents of the attacks on Iraq, that democracy can be installed by military power, is like something from a different universe for me. This is not an anti-American attitude. I am essentially very pro-American, I greatly appreciate American society, its style of life and its optimistic pragmatism, but even in the United States, the Right leads a fundamental dispute about this war. A significant portion of it does not approve of the military solution and claims that President Bush breaches and damages the conservative ideals of a free America with this foreign-policy foray.

Then there are the problems into which the international community will get when the war is over, when it attempts to create a new Iraq, cut out according to a western pattern. *Democracy may be supported and inspired, but we cannot dictate it to anyone, and even less so by military force.* And not only that. If this model of exporting democracy is to become the norm, who will be its next object? And who will put together the list of countries? And where is it all going to end? Will it still be that free world for which we strive, and whose ideals are also, or even primarily, American ideals?

I cannot evaluate in detail the current danger connected with the possible or probable Iraqi ownership of weapons of mass destruction. Beyond all doubt, there are a number of other countries about which we may rightfully presume something similar, or about which we even already know it. Mechanisms must be created which would prevent anyone — including terrorists — from using those weapons, or which would at least make their use difficult, and minimize the potential consequences. This is a huge and complex undertaking for the entire international community. It is definitely not possible to launch a massive, comprehensive preventive war.

And another personal note. My opinions in this respect are of a permanent and consistent nature. I did not hide them when I held my previous political posts. I have always expressed them publicly, and I have always tried to gain political support for them, although it often cost me significant "political points." *As the president of the country I repeat that I find the current Czech — not American, not French — attitude of the government and Parliament balanced.* That is something significantly different than just a witticism, as some commentators tried to present this attitude. A politician must be brave and able to "blow against the wind," if he is convinced of it. I know that well, but at the same time, I am honored that my opinions, feelings and attitudes correlate with the majority attitude of the Czech public. In matters as fatal as war and peace, the need for a fundamental agreement between the political representation and the public is always the principal thing. And, after all, American presidents have always known something about that.

Europe, the Global Economy and the United States

Munich Economic Summit, Munich, Hotel Bayerischer Hof, May 2, 2003

I am pleased and honored to be here today and to have the opportunity to address this distinguished audience. Before starting, I have to say that this is my first speech abroad in my new function, with the exception of speeches at presidential dinners during my first foreign trips. I intend to participate in conferences like this one, which means I have to find an uneasy and risky position somewhere between official presentations short on ideas and strong views and careless or carefree academic talks full of thought-provoking ideas. I am not sure I will succeed in finding such a position, but I will do my best.

This year's Munich Economic Summit has in its title three words: Europe, global economy, and United States. I shall briefly touch on each of them.

In Athens two weeks ago, I signed on behalf of the Czech Republic the Accession Treaty to the European Union. I would like to add a few words to it. We all know that, for a long time, Europe was a divided continent. We who lived in its eastern part know this even better.

The collapse of communism more than 13 years ago eliminated one of Europe's most important dividing lines, the Iron Curtain, and this helped to put into motion a dramatic process of opening-up, liberalizing and deregulating Central and Eastern European societies. All of them underwent a radical transition from communism to the system of political democracy and a market economy. Despite many difficulties, we have, by and large, year after year, seen progress. Now, I dare to say, in their basic political and economic structures and institutions, the Central and Eastern European countries are already close to the countries which were lucky not to fall into the communist trap.

Western Europe — finally and with visible hesitation — recognized their progress by offering them membership in the European Union. The ex-communist countries accepted it because they wanted to be normal European countries, which nowadays is impossible without EU membership. That was the main basis for their motivation to enter the EU as soon as possible. They asked for it even if they knew that the nominal, institutional convergence (the acceptance of *acquis communautaire* and of other "parameters" and policies connected with membership) in many respects blocks or postpones the needed real convergence.

The Czech Republic is ready to participate in the European integration process and to carry out all the necessary requirements connected with the membership. We have a feeling, however, that there is a discrepancy between what we get and what we give. The economic effects of the elimination of all kinds of barriers (of liberalization in a broad sense) have been — in my understanding — more advantageous for the current member countries than for us. We hope that the continuous evolutionary process of real convergence will finally bring about a balance between costs and benefits, but it will take a longer time than is usually expected.

This is further complicated by the fact that Europe faces a big challenge these days. It has to guarantee genuine freedom and liberal democracy (in the classical sense) to the people of the continent as well as create an efficient market economy. I am afraid that both freedom and efficiency have been reduced by the developments of the last few years or decades. It makes me nervous that Europe is not sufficiently aware of these dangers and lives in a nirvana of relative affluence, of vacations spent in the pleasant climates of the South, of the nonexistence of authoritarian or totalitarian regimes on its soil, of several decades of peace and positive economic growth. We should be aware of the fragility and vulnerability of all that. Instead, European politicians are preoccupied with building a continental entity which aims at the formation of a postmodernist, postnational, postdemocratic, multicultural pan-European state and the elimination of traditional European nation-states. I may be wrong in seeing our future this way but I am definitely not the only one who does.

To be correctly understood, I do not criticize the more or less spontaneous European integration process (if it is only modestly institutionally supported), but I do criticize its current unionistic and heavily institutionalized character. The difference between those two ways of organizing the continent is not sufficiently exposed to the citizens of European countries and the "unionists" or "federalists" try to blur (not to "Blair") the obvious and substantial difference. They evidently aim at establishing a compact European superstate. They try to sell it, however, with a different title — as an opening up of the European continent, as a method for guaranteeing peace, as a way to ensure the free movement of people, goods and services, money and capital, ideas and cultural patterns around Europe. This is a project I will always defend and support — together with them.

I do not believe we can continue without reforming the current approach. Many of us believe that genuine democracy cannot be established (and maintained) in an entity bigger than a state. Or, to put it differently, we do not see any source of democratic legitimacy higher than the constitutional democratic state. Many Europeans speak about the EU's democratic deficit, which is — in my understanding — a substitute for saying that the EU is run by unelected bureaucrats, by predominantly "internationally" motivated politicians and by the belief in the advantages of the majority voting schemes at a continental level. We have to ask ourselves whether it is possible to imagine the development of genuinely democratic international institutions at that level. For me, only states give people a sense of identity and provide a framework for individual freedom. The current Convention should face such issues straight-on, without escaping to less relevant ones. The Europeans deserve it and our good, old Europe deserves it as well.

The opening up of societies all over the world goes on and, more and more, the so-called global economy becomes a reality. It has some pleasant and some unpleasant consequences. Competition in an increasingly "borderless" world grows and will keep growing. Only efficient, flexible, forward-looking firms will survive. How will the European firms do? There is no doubt that the people of Europe belong to the same category — sometimes caricatured as *homo oeconomicus* — as people of any other continent. They do not need to be either reeducated or masterminded by the missionaries (or perhaps mercenaries) of globalization. They need something else. They need liberal economic and social policies. They need a new wave of deregulation and liberalization. They need the restructuring and stabilization of public finances, of pension systems, of health systems, of social security systems, of industrial and agricultural policies, of antimonopolistic and competition policies, etc.

Europe is characterized — not accidentally — by high mandatory costs imposed by government paternalism and regulation. The demand for them belongs to the category of luxury goods, which means it grows faster than income. There exists, however, an unpleasant tradeoff between costs and growth of income. At some level the high costs start to slow down the growth of incomes and a very unpleasant vicious circle begins. Various economic studies demonstrate that this is what happened to Europe and what goes on despite political promises to stop it. Europe has, I am afraid, no other way out than to rapidly react. The efficient, low-cost firms in the rest of the world are not waiting for us and there is no doubt that there will be more of them in the near future. Globalization, whatever the word means, will continue and eventually gain momentum. We have to accept it and to react.

The United States has a much more liberal economy and a less heavy social system than Europe. This country is consistently more antistatist, individualistic, laissez faire (and because of its dynamics, even egalitarian) than other democracies. This is what produces its wealth and strength. We need to maintain a functioning transatlantic relationship for many reasons, but for me the most important reason is its role in enabling a transatlantic transfer of ideas and ideologies, of lifestyles and cultural patterns, of work ethic and workaholism, of courage and decisiveness. The currently fashionable European anti-Americanism, the caricaturing of American life and culture, and Europe's incapacity for an open and therefore risky dialogue, are frustrating phenomena. I tried to oppose them for a long time but without success. Let's talk. Civility requires a willingness to listen to others. We should start a serious dialogue because this is the only way to increase understanding on both sides. Saying that does not imply that all of us must be happy with the American handling of the Iraqi crisis, but even in this case we should start talking and listening to one another. Listening is the most scarce good these days. I am glad the Munich Economic Summit makes talking and listening possible.

Old Europe, New Europe and New Anti-Americanism

World Forum, American Enterprise Institute, Beaver Creek, Colorado, June 20, 2003

To have a serious dialogue between Europe and America is of extraordinary importance. Especially now, the Beaver Creek World Forum is almost indispensable. It is our mutual task to destroy various myths and misunderstandings, both old and new ones, created by our predecessors or by us, based on fair or unfair evaluations of events, on words or deeds, on authentic or only assumed positions, etc.

As someone from Europe, I have the feeling that Europe is historically a less homogeneous entity than America. It is, therefore, more ambiguous to make generalizations about Europe than about America. There are differences in Europe but I have problems with the currently stressed distinction between old and new Europe and I will try to say why.

We here, this morning, are speakers from four different parts of Europe. We came here with our own genuine interests. We have our priorities, loyalties, historical experiences, memories and fears. Our geographical positions are different, as well as to some respect our minds and thoughts.

1. Having mentioned historical experiences — some of us have more than enough reasons not to take freedom for granted. We are aware of its fragility and its enemies. We know that freedom is neither a gift nor an export commodity. We are sensitive to the slightest signs of its violations. We, therefore, stress the right to have views and to stand by them.

Our communist past was an important lesson. To talk about freedom and its implications at that time was not a free academic discourse without consequences. We understood that to have freedom and to be free meant many things. It requires the courage to express unorthodox and nonconformist views, the ability to listen to unpleasant opinions and the willingness to engage in an open dialogue. This experience may be one of the relevant European differences but it has no connection with geography, with "the age of countries" or with EU membership.

2. Having mentioned loyalties — we know something about the relative importance of external pressures (as compared to domestic factors) in bringing about a systemic change — in our case, dismantling communism. We know that the breakdown of the Berlin Wall as well as the outbreak of our Velvet

Revolution were not made possible by German *Ostpolitik* or by détente, but because of the strong stances of Ronald Reagan and Margaret Thatcher. And we know who was really instrumental in our entry into NATO, which we value so highly. This feeling of loyalty gives us a clearly defined corridor to walk. It does not turn us into rope-walkers who have absolutely no degree of freedom to choose our behavior in individual cases.

3. Having mentioned interests — in the past some of us, as individuals and as countries, were frustrated by being forced to neglect our national interests and instead to promote the interests of "the world proletariat" or of the Soviet Union Communist Party Politburo. Now we would like to be able to defend our own interests (something that is, I suppose, in the best traditions of the American foreign policy doctrine). We would prefer doing it without being labeled "old" or "new" while doing it. I believe it is a fair request. We are aware of the importance of keeping the transatlantic ties strong, we value the significance of NATO in the post-Cold war era, and we know that individual freedoms and liberties as well as national and cultural identities must be actively defended. However, our national interests should continue to be defined by us and we should follow them.

It was easier to be united against the threat of the Soviet Union than now, in the era of less transparent and less tangible dangers. Once the constraints of the Cold War were lifted, the interests of individual countries in what we call the West have started to break up and will continue to do so.

What about the so-called anti-Americanism? I usually warn against labeling because it dangerously simplifies issues. Nevertheless, the term "New Anti-Americanism" seems to be quite inspiring because it automatically evokes the idea of an Old Anti-Americanism. I have been one of the strongest critics of what we now call an old European anti-Americanism. I have always admired the American political, social and economic systems. I have always disagreed with the unfair trivializations of American culture. I was a diligent student of American economic and social sciences. I appreciated American convictions, mode of life, individualist and rationalist culture, pragmatism, work habits, efficiency, simplicity of behavior, optimism, etc. In addition, I opposed those European intellectuals who tried to explain September 11 as a reaction to American capitalism and to the "McDonaldization" of the rest of the world, which would — without it — live in a Rousseau-like innocent paradise.

However, I have to admit that I don't know exactly what the adjective "new" refers to. The various doubts about the Iraq War and only conditional or partial participation in the war itself must not be regarded as an anti-Americanism — either old or new. Would it not be un-American to look at it in such a way? We have to carefully distinguish between friendly and constructive criticism and explicit and planned hostility. Even now, I see in Europe much more of the first than of the second. Our American friends should know it. Not recognizing this important distinction leads sometimes to what I call not New, but New-New Anti-Americanism which appears in Europe these days among the former active opponents of an old anti-Americanism. This is, I believe, something we must not accept.

Freedom and Its Enemies (as Seen from Central Europe)

Freedom Lecture, Woodrow Willson Center, Washington, D.C., November 19, 2003

I agree with one of my gurus, Friedrich von Hayek, that "freedom cannot endure unless every generation restates and reemphasizes its value." I would extend his argument slightly by saying that these days such a restatement should be done also by those who lived for decades in a nonfree communist world. The reason for it is clear and straightforward. They were, paradoxically, enriched by their life in such a regime and they therefore don't take freedom for granted. They are sensitive to all kinds of creeping, for other people almost invisible, changes, which signal to them the future possibility of the weakening (and the potential loss) of freedom in the nominally free (because formally nontotalitarian) world.

I disagree with those who minimize or explicitly deny our comparative advantage in this respect, who assume that we should still be taught only what freedom really means and should not try to give warnings to those who have lived only in a free society. On one hand we were impoverished by our life in the communist society, we may be biased, we may underestimate some important things, but on the other we have a unique experience which should not be forgotten. I agree with the first Freedom Lecture speaker Michael Novak that, "looking ahead to the 21st century, the problem that worries me most is the fragility of free societies."[13] I see many symptoms of freedom-weakening attitudes, initiatives and activities, and am convinced that they should be taken seriously. What follows is a brief summary of my position on those issues.

1. The Current Expansion of Attitudes Endangering Freedom

After decades spent in a collectivistic society, people like me believe more than those who were privileged not to go through this experience in the primacy of the individual and are, therefore, frustrated by a growing pressure to place individual rights and responsibilities below and behind group rights and entitlements. This is these days considered in the West to be modern, progressive and politically correct — even if it undoubtedly directly endangers both individual freedom and human liberty.

Together with Michael Novak, I believe in the centrality of freedom and of human liberty as well as of democracy, and am afraid when this is being denied or overlooked. It has many forms. The proponents of Third Ways such as

Anthony Giddens (see his "The Third Way and Its Critics") suddenly fight for "the democratization of democracy," which is a radically different concept and project than freedom. We don't need a redefinition or reinterpretation of the basic terms of classical liberalism because the original — which means uninnovated — idea of freedom, liberty, democracy and capitalism "is powerful and sufficiently robust." However, "it must be continuously exposed, explained and defended."[14] Otherwise it becomes forgotten or stolen (and filled with different meanings).

As I said, we believe in the classical understanding of freedom and are not in favor of unnecessary and often contradictory innovations. I don't see the now fashionable ideology of human rights (not to speak about activist and radical "human rightism") to be a neutral and innocent concept. I see in it an alternative, purposefully rather fuzzy ideology and a political doctrine.

The same is true about markets. We believe in free markets, not in dreams about the convergence of economic systems, or in the corporate social responsibility doctrine, which represents another attempt to control, regulate and mastermind markets. The danger connected with this is not understood by the government, by trade unions, by NGOs or by leading representatives of corporations because they are, as Milton Friedman correctly stated, "pro-business, not pro-market." Our experience with central planning and state ownership warns us against putting social responsibility before economic rationality, against misunderstandings of the philosophical and systemic implications of economic science.

We believe in the primacy of human beings, not in slogans like "Earth First," nor in the seductive concept of sustainable development, which is a misleading concept. It puts ahead neither nature nor the quality of environment, but immodest constructivistic ambitions of those who want to gain control of all of us. They use nature and environment as their "hostages," which is successful because we all place nature and environment very high on our list of priorities.

We are against all kinds of discrimination because we know what discrimination is, but we cannot accept the currently popular principle of nondiscrimination. It reminds us of an almost Jacobinical principle of absolute equality, which is — as history teaches us — an opposite to freedom. We consider the people to be "natural equals" and consistently distinguish formal equality of opportunity from substantive equality of results. For a long time, we were dreaming about life in the First World but had to live in the Second. We know as well that it established an enormous degree of inequality in our societies. This second concept is reflected in requirements to guarantee "equality before the law, equality under the law, and equal benefit of the law."[15] This substantive equality concept is in many circles heralded as a new era of social progressiveness and is connected with "the premise that government is ultimately a benevolent force, obliged to guarantee equal outcomes by redistributing benefits and privileges between individuals and groups."[16] We know that it does not work that way.

We all undoubtedly see the importance of morality for the functioning of a human "great society" (as compared to simple "face-to-face" societies), but we are against the rhetoric of moral righteousness on the side of public intellectuals, of the anointed (in the terminology of Thomas Sowell),[17] of the Olympians (in the terminology of Robert H. Bork),[18] because we feel in it the strong authoritarian temper of those who want to impose their values on others. They pretend to know better than the rest of us what we need and what we want. And what is good for us. They want to protect us from ourselves. Antonio Martino once said that "we are heading towards a society where pedestrians will be required to have a license, obesity will be illegal and what we are allowed to eat will be determined by the National Dieting Board."[19] I don't take these words as science fiction, I see them already around. We don't want, however, to be protected from ourselves. For us "at the heart of liberty is the right to define one's own concepts of existence, of meaning, of the universe, and of the mystery of human life."[20]

Another danger comes from judicial activism (or judicial imperialism, as it is called by Robert H. Bork), which leads to "an usurpation by judges of powers rightly belonging, in a democracy, to the political branches" of government.[21] This issue relates to the topics of judicial accountability, judicial activism or judicial restraint, and individual or group freedoms. I agree with Neil Seeman that "judicial activism, when it undermines parliamentary intent, is necessarily antidemocratic, since it elevates the judiciary to the role of political actor capable of usurping the political process"[22] and I am afraid that "it signifies a deeply troubling democracy gap."[23]

It seems to me as well that we are witnesses to the crowding out of standard democratic methods by alternative political procedures based on communitarianism, NGOism, and corporativism. Gresham's Law is valid here no less than in the sphere of currency where it was discovered. The alternative procedures are worse than the original ones. Because of that, political power moves into the hands of rent-seeking coalitions, of various pressure groups and of vested interest institutions. It creates a new feudalization of society (as the term was understood by Ludwig Erhard in Germany in the '70s).

Another dimension of freedom-weakening activities lies in attempts to suppress the role of national states and to internationalize issues. It leads to the undermining of standard democratic accountability, which exists in national states. But this is not my special topic here today. It will certainly be possible to expand this list of un- or anti-freedom attitudes, but the real danger is in their synergy. It is made possible by the activities of a very wide coalition of antimarket, antibourgeois, antifreedom, elitist scribes and intellectuals. We should pay attention to their motives.

2. The Causes of Such Attitudes

I see three basic groups of causes. They are based on ideas, interests and fears.

As regards ideas, the main influence is the belief in the market failure doctrine accompanied by the presumption that politically organized correction for market failures would work perfectly. This is what all kinds of socialists repeat again and again. It is, however, wrong. As James Buchanan puts it: "market failures were set against an idealized politics," which is an incorrect comparison.[24] This idealist theory of the state has been in past decades successfully criticized by the Public Choice School of Buchanan and Tullock and by many other thinkers, but it is still with us. The serious analysis of the behavior of persons acting politically — voters, politicians or bureaucrats — has not succeeded in rejecting the romantic mythology of the state and of the motivations and possibilities of politicians and their bureaucrats. I agree with Buchanan that the public is now "more critical about politics and politicians, more cynical about the motivation of political action, and less naive in thinking that political nostrums offer easy solutions to social problems" than half a century ago, but the old dreams are still there.[25] Even the failure of socialism did not bring about a collapse and disappearance of this set of ideas. The Hayekian "fatal conceit" remains to govern the world of ideas and brings a lot of people into the camp of statism.

Some people are personally motivated to be in favor of a different world rather than a free society (in the classical liberal meaning of the term) because they hope they will gain from it.[26] They hope there will be a demand for their activities there. A centrally organized, regulated and controlled society offers an enormous opportunity for some people to give ideas, advice and recommendations. By doing this they can reconstruct the world according to their own ideas and at the same time be paid for it. My favorite American public philosopher, Eric Hoffer, said in 1977 in a similar argument: "There are quite a number of people who have a vested interest in the stuff and make a noble living out of it." This is true and well-known in many societies and historical periods but the most visible recent example is the new European political, bureaucratic and even intellectual institution, the European Union. Its formation and expansion is accompanied by a huge demand for ideas, advice, defense and justification (of its existence). The real motivation for the deepening and widening of the EU is different from the nominal interpretation of it. Interest and especially self-interest is more important than the ideas.

Finally, there is a fear. Fear of those who don't believe in themselves, who are afraid of openness, of freedom, of markets, of competition, who hope that someone else will help them, will take care of them, will be responsible for them, who believe in the rhetoric of those who promise them a life without full responsibility for it. I don't speak about those who are really weak, ill, old, handicapped (they do need our help) but about those who are willing to substitute the paternalistic state for freedom and responsibility. In their attitudes, they are — perhaps unconsciously — significant supporters of the anointed, of the Olympians, of the advocates of the state and interventionism. Without those who are afraid of freedom the success of statists would not be possible.

It is our task to understand and explain the impact of this special coalition of ideas, interests and fears and to come with a clear, straightforward and feasible alternative. It must be based on the return to the classical liberalism.

Address Delivered by President Václav Klaus on the Occasion of the Fifth Anniversary of Czech Membership in NATO

Prague Castle, March 12, 2004

Today we celebrate the fifth anniversary of an event of extraordinary importance for our country. Exactly five years ago the Czech Republic became a full-fledged member of the North Atlantic Alliance. We have thus fulfilled one of the chief foreign policy goals of our renewed democracy, which was to anchor the Czech Republic firmly in the defense and security structures of the free world and to secure our free and democratic national existence through a union with the strongest defense alliance in history, led by the United States. This step formally ended the period of uncertainty and the security vacuum that emerged in Central Europe after the fall of communism. Having taken this step, our country has returned — this time hopefully for good — to the core of the western world where we belonged before the communist era.

NATO membership was a priority for our country since the fall of communism, a priority nobody even questioned. That is why we emphasized it so much. That is why we rejected at the beginning of the 1990s ideas that played with the unrealistic vision of our country becoming a sort of a "bridge" between the East and West, illusions resembling those that repeatedly contributed to our fall into totalitarian regimes in the past. That is why we so resolutely rejected the suggestion that NATO should be dissolved together with the Warsaw Pact.

The North Atlantic Alliance has been indispensable in securing the stability, security and prosperity of the European continent. Besides being a substantially defensive and military structure, the alliance also plays the role — even more importantly for us — of a vital institutional warranty of the transatlantic relationship between Europe and the United States on the political but also generally cultural and civilization level. The presence of the United States has been crucial in the enforcement and stabilization of democracy and civil and economic liberties on the European continent in the past 50 years. I am convinced these transatlantic ties should remain strong and functional, and not only in the sphere of defense, at the beginning of the 21st century. The NATO membership of the Czech Republic, Poland and Hungary as well as the following absorption of other postcommunist countries undoubtedly further strengthened the importance of the Alliance as the crucial European defense structure. And from this point of view we assess some of the current ambitious plans of building more or less independent European defense structures that do not correspond with the interpretation of the transatlantic bond as I understand it.

The incorporation of the Czech Republic in the Alliance also became a significant impetus for the transformation of our armed forces. The capability to fulfill our obligations and to be a fully operational component of the Alliance forces belongs among the main objectives of our military reform even though, and I wish to emphasize this, it is not our only goal. We do not build our military exclusively as expeditionary forces or as a mere support structure of Alliance forces. We want to be a full-fledged ally capable of securing the dominant role in the country's defense and capable of operations abroad. We do not want to be a "free rider" and I am convinced we have proved this determination through our participation in several foreign missions.

In the course of the five years that have passed since our accession to NATO, much has changed in the world; many new and unexpected threats have emerged. That is why NATO is now also facing the task of its own transformation. Yet, even this period has confirmed the continuing importance and meaning of the alliance between Europe and the U.S.A. Thus we consider the smooth functioning of the Alliance to be one of our key national interests. We are fully aware of this and it would be good if our partners in the Alliance knew it as well.

NATO and Today's World

North Atlantic Treaty Organization Summit, Istanbul, June 28, 2004

Secretary General, distinguished colleagues, ladies and gentlemen, we are meeting in a rather complicated international situation, which forces us to face new challenges, to solve new tasks, to fulfill new obligations. It also brings new risks. We have to discuss them and I believe our intention is to find maximum understanding if not unity among us.

Not everything is, however, new today. The Alliance demonstrated its readiness to cope with many new phenomena and the result was a significant step forward at the Prague summit two years ago. We can, therefore, afford not to make substantial innovations here today. This does not mean of course that we should stay where we are, without moving ahead.

It was a very good decision to organize the present summit here in Turkey, in the neighborhood of the Middle East, one of the major sources of conflicts, terrorism and instability in today's world. The choice of the place suggests that we all regard this region as a priority in the pursuit of our interests. I can assure you the Czech Republic also sees international terrorism associated with this region as one of the main security problems of the day. And although international terrorism is a relatively new, different and highly specific threat, one that is very difficult to get rid of using traditional means of military defense, the Czech Republic firmly believes that NATO should play a key role also in this matter.

I do believe the present summit will bring us a step forward; I do believe it will help to clarify our tasks; I do believe the present summit will result in a deeper understanding of the causes of international terrorism, and in a more accurate definition of it, because the word "terrorism" should not become a political magic formula which could absorb anything; I believe the summit will contribute to the rebuilding of unity of views among the member states of the Alliance based on a serious political dialogue which we have a chance to lead here; I believe that the summit will result in the further strengthening of the transatlantic link, that NATO — as the only functional defense structure in today's world — will continue to play that role in the future, that it will remain the base of security for Europe and that all the recent and future initiatives aimed at building a European defense entity will be put into harmony with NATO.

It is our obligation to make sure that NATO and the European Security and Defense Policy will be complementary, that a positive synergy will be achieved, that competition, duplication of structures, loss of unity and coherence will be avoided. Development of an alternative defense and security structure on the European continent should be prevented.

NATO must retain its traditional military defense nature rather than be gradually transformed into a loosely defined institution of collective security, more similar to the Organization for Security and Cooperation in Europe or UN peacekeeping forces than to its original form. It must not happen that in crises — as it sometimes happens to those organizations — NATO enters late, without having realistically prepared political solutions, without clear prospects of terminating the conflict, with the risk of a long-term engagement. The Olympic Games in Athens this summer is a good example of a mission which has a different meaning than a traditional military defense one. I think we should think twice about such missions in the future.

I am convinced that this summit in Istanbul will give another important impetus to the Alliance and will further develop the changes initiated at the Prague summit. Looking at it from our own perspective, the basis for this is the maintenance of the transatlantic defense link, which was the main guarantee for Europe's 50 years of peace. We stand firmly for its continuation.

Notes for BOAO Forum for Asia

Hainan, China, April 24, 2004

Let me express my gratitude for the invitation which I have gladly accepted to participate in this important gathering. It gives the president of a small Central European country a very good opportunity to present the Czech Republic to the political and business leaders of China, of Southeast Asia and of the whole Asian continent. I would like to assure you that we consider our political, economic, social and cultural presence in your region to be a very significant aspect of our activities. After the collapse of communism, already almost 15 years ago, our ambition was to go "back to Europe," by which we had in mind to become a "normal" European country after half a century of living in a different world. I was, however, always in a hurry to add that in reality it meant going "back to the rest of the world." We wanted to be a free and open country and I believe that we have succeeded in this uneasy endeavor.

As some of you may know, in six days, on the first of May, the Czech Republic will become a full member of the European Union, which will be a totally new stage in the thousand-year-old history of the country. We will lose a non-negligible part of our sovereignty, but we will have a chance to participate in this very innovative experiment — to organize society without using the standard mechanisms of the nation-state. We are aware of the costs and benefits as well as of risks of such an experiment and I have to say that we are not extremely optimistic in this respect. We are, however, determined to use this new opportunity to accelerate the economic and social development of Czech society. We hope as well that our membership in the EU will be interpreted in your region as a proof of our maturity, of our stability, of the success in our radical transition from communism to a free, pluralistic society and market economy.

The overwhelming and far-reaching transition of the Czech Republic, which started immediately after the collapse of communism, is over. All inevitable reform measures were taken during the first decade of the postcommunist era and the current stage of our development can already be described as an almost uneventful evolution of the quality of important political, economic and social institutions as well as of the strengths, depths and robustness of political and economic markets. Many changes and improvements are needed, but the need for such reforms is no greater than in "old" EU member states.

After several decades of life in a more or less closed and semiautarchic society we are strong believers in the importance of openness, of free markets and of the free flow of ideas, news, human beings, skills and technologies, goods and services, money and capital as well as culture all over the world. We are convinced that such elements of globalization increase prosperity and benefit all who participate.

We want to be visible in your region and — reciprocally — we invite all of you to do business with us and to invest in the Czech Republic. I brought with me on my 10-day trip to China a group of successful Czech businessmen and I hope they have used this opportunity to strengthen the already established contacts, to make new ones and to find new partners. I hope the stay here at the BOAO Forum for Asia will be useful in this respect as well.

The fast economic reconstruction and modernization of China and of Southeast Asia as a whole is in our part of the world relatively well-known. I myself was prepared for this trip by my past visits in the region as well as by my extensive reading about it. I, therefore, expected that no expectations-reality gap would arise during my trip. I was wrong. In most human activities, the expectations usually exceed reality and the people become disappointed. This is not the case in this region. The reality exceeds the expectations. I am really glad to be here with you.

Gulliver Tied Down

Response to an Essay by Charles Krauthammer, 2004

The events of recent years, the terrorist attack in New York and its counterpart, the war in Iraq, dramatized the already existing arguments about the very essence of the current international political system and about the interpretation of the behavior of the most important and strongest country within that system, the United States. This debate is accompanied by many misunderstandings, accusations, falsifications, mistrust, but also by a "shadow-playing" of politicians, which, unfortunately, obscures and complicates the true substance of the matter.

It is, therefore, particularly valuable when somebody takes a look at this issue from a different point of view, when he comes clean and calls a spade a spade with the advantage of a nonpolitician's perspective. We are offered this opportunity by reading a brief 20-page booklet, published in the spring of 2004 by the American Enterprise Institute for Public Policy Research, without doubt the most influential contemporary American think tank. The book contains the speech of Charles Krauthammer, prominent American journalist, Pulitzer Prize winner, given on the occasion of his acceptance of the prestigious Irving Kristol Prize, awarded once a year by this institute. The title of his essay is "Democratic Realism: An American Foreign Policy for a Unipolar World." We could not have any clearer words by an American speaker.

The author begins by stating that on December 26, 1991 — and he adds, without a single shot fired, without a revolution and without even a press release — the Soviet Union was finished, died, disappeared. This was, in his eyes, an absolutely "inhuman system that, like other genetically defective organisms, expired in its sleep," leaving America "global dominance" and at the same time the question of "how to deal with it."[26]

Krauthammer distinguishes among four principal American opinions on how to cope with this dominance:

1. Isolationism, which, however, Krauthammer strongly refuses as a totally lifeless, intellectually obsolete and politically bankrupt view and for these reasons, he doesn't consider it in detail at all;

2. Liberal internationalism, which Krauthammer designates as the foreign political doctrine of American Democrats and their spiritual kin among foreign political elites. In his opinion, the prototype of the application of this position is Clinton's presidency and his so called "humanitarian interventionism" (Somalia, Haiti, Bosnia, Kosovo), which is acceptable for its proponents only on the condition that it is devoid of any promotion of American national interests in places where it intervenes militarily. The consequence of the American Democrats' position is the defense of multilateralism and "mania for international treaties" and "obsession with conventions, protocols, legalisms," whose sole aim is — in Krauthammer's opinion — to temper American power and force and "reduce American freedom of acting by making it subservient to, dependent on, constricted by the will and interests of other nations." The whole point of multilateralism is only one: "to tie down Gulliver with a thousand strings." This analogy is the key idea of the text — Krauthammer feels that the United States is Gulliver, and he doesn't want to be tied down in any way by anybody;

3. A doctrine called realism seems to be for him more acceptable. Realism considers efforts at the democratization of foreign political systems as a "hopeless illusion" because it "requires a revolution in human nature." That is what the realists obviously not only do not want, but even consider impossible. Krauthammer shares with them the fundamental refusal of the whole concept of "international community" used by liberal internationalists. It is not a community, it is a cacophony! That is why in the unipolar world of today, world stability is secured solely and exclusively by "the overwhelming power and deterrent threat of the United States." Only U.S. power "protects civilization from barbarism." That is to say "realists choose not to be Gullivers;"

4. But Krauthammer realizes that this is not enough, because it is not possible to "live by power alone." We need ideas, too. Therefore, he subscribes to *democratic globalism,* which he designates as the Bush Administration's foreign policy doctrine. This approach represents the conservative alternative to realism. It is based on a "definition of national interests not as a power, but as values," bearing in mind that the "supreme value is the success of liberty." On the basis of this doctrine, history is interpreted as a perpetual duel between freedom and nonfreedom, good and evil. Realism lacks a vision, whereas democratic globalism has one — it is freedom, democracy and goodness.

This way of structuring the topic and laying out its clear contours is extremely useful, because it makes discussion and analysis possible. But I would like to raise a few questions, my answers to which do not correspond with those of Charles Krauthammer:

- Is it possible for all of us to accept the idea that the task of a dominant superpower is in "shaping the international environment by projecting power abroad to secure economic, political, and strategic goods" anywhere in the world?
- Can we accept the idea that in the unipolar world of today America is "a supreme central authority wielding a monopoly of power and enforcing norms"? Even further, that America should have a monopoly on enforcing correct norms of conduct in the whole world?
- Should we swallow the explicit formulation that only America, only and exclusively, "is the land mine between barbarism and civilization"? Is that land mine only and exclusively the U.S.A.?
- Is it right to interpret the contemporary world as "a world of terrorists, rogue states and weapons of mass destruction"? Is just that the fundamental characteristic of the contemporary world?
- Does it result from the previous that for the dominant power "preemption is the only possible strategy"? Any time? Anywhere?
- Does America have the right to be "the arbiter of international events" and "custodian of the international system?" Would it not be sufficient that America would seek to diffuse and advertise its views, positions, norms and values?

Even though I cannot — in the best of my conscience — answer these questions in an absolutely affirmative way, there are various other interesting things in this text. I also find in Krauthammer a lot of strong ideas which I share and which are so clearly expressed by just a few others apart from him. These include:

- Resolute refusal to justify Clinton-Albright's "humanitarian interventionism;"
- Denounciation of the emptiness and flatness of multilateral treaties and organizations (that are increasing in geometric progression);
- Polemic with the affirmation that "multilateral action has a higher moral standing" than a unilateral action only and solely owing to this multilateral character (like in the case of the war in Iraq with or without the permission of the UN);

- Disapproval of the tendency among American (and also our own) liberals to reject any argument based on national interests;
- Critique of liberals' erroneous premise that it is possible "to remake the international system in the image of domestic civil society;"
- Attack upon the fictitiousness of the idea of existence of something that is called an international community;
- Thesis that realism without a vision is insufficient, etc., etc.

We can thank the author for his essay, but let us keep our doubts whether Gulliver himself always knows best what he should do and what is good for others.

Notes for U.S. Independence Day Speech 2004

U. S. Embassy, Prague, July 2, 2004

Mr. Ambassador, Ladies and Gentlemen, dear American friends,

I feel honored to be asked by the Ambassador of the United States, this time by Ambassador Cabaniss, to say a few words here on this very special occasion as a representative of the Czech Republic.

Mr. Ambassador, all of us are pleased and honored to be invited to be here today and to have the opportunity to celebrate the 228th Independence Day of the United States of America together with you. I can assure you that in recent years the Fourth of July has been a firm and fixed point in our annual calendar of events. I am sure you know it was not always the case in this country. In the past we were forced to remember other events.

Today we celebrate — and I am not sure whether to say already or only — the 15th Independence Day in a free Czech Republic. I repeat again and again that we know who helped us get rid of the oppressive communist regime.

Mr. Ambassador, three weeks ago I visited your country. I was privileged to participate in the funeral of your great president, Ronald Reagan, whose role in ending communism not only in this country, but worldwide, was enormous. Some of us were aware of that already during his presidency, the rest — I believe — were able to understand it during the last 15 years.

Communism is over but our concern about freedom and our fight for freedom here and elsewhere is and should be never-ending. Communism is, however, not the only problem. We see the appearance of new "isms" and of new dangerous attempts to suppress freedom. The tragedy of September 11 showed us that we are not at the end of history, that we do not live in the world of all-embracing tolerance, with no dictatorships, with no wars and with no human suffering. Three days ago I returned from the NATO summit in Istanbul and would like to stress how impressed I was by the very high degree of mutual understanding of the dangers undermining our freedom, our democracy, our political and economic stability, among political leaders of NATO countries.

Mr. Ambassador, as you know, two month ago we became members of the European Union. We did it because we wanted to participate in the — in principle, positive — European integration process. Its current form is, however, a problem and an important challenge for us. I would like to assure you that the Czech Republic will not forget the importance of transatlantic cooperation and will not let anyone weaken our friendship with your great country. I would also like to assure you that I believe that we will overcome the present political crisis, connected with the resignation of the government, and especially that our foreign policy will not be affected by the change of government.

I wish the American people a lot of success, prosperity and peace. Thank you for inviting us to share this special day with you.

Footnotes to Chapter IV

[1] Winston Churchhill speech given September 19, 1946, Zurich, Switzerland; see David Cannadine, ed. *Blood, Toll, Tears and Sweat: The Speeches of Winston Churchill* (Boston: Houghton Mifflin, 1989).

[2] G. Radnitzky, "The Inconsistency of Liberal Compromises," *Journal des Economistes et des Etudes Humaines*, Vol. 7, No. 4., December 1996.

[3] Rose Friedman and Milton Friedman, *Two Lucky People* (University of Chicago Press, 1998).

[4] Henry G. Manne, "The Judiciary and Free Markets," *Harvard Journal of Law and Public Policy*, Vol. 21, No. 1, Fall 1997.

[5] Joseph Stiglitz, "Development Based on Participation — A Strategy for Transforming Societies," in *Transition*, Vol. 9, No. 6, December 1998, World Bank.

[6] Norman Barry, "There is No Philadelphia in Europe," *The Freeman*, Vol. 49, No. 2, February 1999, Foundation for Economic Education.

[7] *The Washington Post*, September 27, 1998.

[8] See my speech on Ludwig Erhard, reprinted in Václav Klaus, *Tschechische* Transformation und *europäische* Integration (Passau: Neue Presse Verlag, 1995).

[9] Wilhelm Roepke, *A Humane Economy* (Intercollegiate Studies Institute, 1998), originally published in 1960.

[10] Kenneth Minogue, *Policy*, No. 1, 1997, Center for Independent Studies, Sydney, Australia.

[11] Anthony Giddens, *The Third Way: The Renewal of Social Democracy* (Cambridge, UK: Policy Press, 1998).

[12] Quoted from Charles Watrin, "Europe's 'New' Third Way," Heritage Lecture No. 634, May 7, 1999, Heritage Foundation.

[13] Michael Novak, *Awakening from Nihilism* (Indianapolis: Crisis Books, 1995), p. 4.

[14] Quotation from my speech at the James Madison Institute Center for World Capitalism in Jacksonville, Florida, 1995.

[15] Criticized by Sylvia LeRoy in "Equality: the Leviathan of Rights," *Fraser Forum*, August 2003, Fraser Institute, p. 21.

[16] Ibid., p. 28.

[17] Thomas Sowell, *The Vision of the Anointed* (New York: Basic Books, 1995).

[18] Robert H. Bork, "Judicial Imperialism," AEI Bradley Lecture, September 2003, American Enterprise Institute.

[19] Antonio Martino, Mont Pelerin Society Meeting in Vienna, in 1996.

[20] Robert H. Bork, "Judicial Imperialism, p. 5.

[21] Ibid, p. 2.

[22] Neil Seeman, "Taking Judicial Activism Seriously," *Fraser Forum*, August 2003, p. 17, Fraser Institute.

[23] Ibid., p. 4.

[24] Jame M. Buchanan, "Public Choice — Politics Without Romance," *Policy*, Vol. 19, No. 3, 2003, p. 16, Center for Independent Studies, Sydney, Australia.

[25] Ibid., p. 17.

[26] See James Buchanan, "Classical Liberalism as an Organizing Ideal," speech at the Mont Pelerin Society Meeting, Chattanooga, Tenn., September 18, 2003.

[27] This and all following quotes are from Charles Krauthammer, "Democratic Realism or An American Foreign Policy for a Unipolar World," February 12, 2004, American Enterprise Institute.

The National Center for Policy Analysis (NCPA) was established in 1983 as a nonprofit, nonpartisan public policy research institute. The NCPA's mission is to develop and promote private alternatives to government regulations and control, solving problems by relying on the strengths of the competitive, entrepreneurial private sector.

The NCPA motto — Making Ideas Change The World — reflects the belief that ideas have enormous power to change the course of human events. The NCPA plays an active role in unleashing that power for positive change by identifying and encouraging the best scholarly research and by aggressively marketing the results of the research.

Working with scholars at colleges, universities and other think tanks, the NCPA focuses on such issues as taxes, health care, crime, welfare, Social Security, Medicare, environmental policy and education reform. The Center's target audience includes policy makers, journalists, business and community leaders and the general public. By producing credible, accurate, timely analyses of public policy options, the NCPA is increasingly providing leadership to the entire public policy community and helping to shape the policy agenda for the 21st century.

The NCPA is customer-focused rather than self-focused. The Center attempts to meet its customers' information needs with the best material available, regardless of who publishes it. The NCPA's electronic newsletter, *Daily Policy Digest,* provides "all that's new in the world of ideas" — summarizing the best research from the entire public policy community. It appears on the NCPA's Internet Web site and is available by e-mail subscription. The NCPA's bimonthly publication, *Executive Alert Extra*, keeps donors informed about all the Center's activites.

Although headquartered in Dallas, the NCPA also has a highly effective Washington, D.C., office that arranges frequent testimony by NCPA experts before congressional committees. This allows the Center to make "outside-the-Beltway" thinking part of Capitol Hill deliberations.

All contributions to the NCPA are tax deductible under Section 501(c)(3) of the Internal Revenue Code. The NCPA accepts no government grants or contracts. The NCPA depends entirely on the financial support of individuals, corporations and foundations.

If you would like to make a donation to the NCPA, please contact the Development Department at:

The National Center for Policy Analysis
12770 Coit Rd., Suite 800
Dallas, Texas 75251
Telephone: 972-386-6272 Fax: 972-386-0924
www.ncpa.org

NCPA Board of Directors

NCPA Chairman
Pete du Pont
Director
Richards, Layton & Finger

John C. Goodman
President
National Center for Policy Analysis

David L. Brennan
Chairman
White Hat Management, LLC

Don A. Buchholz
Chairman of the Board
Southwest Securities, Inc.,
Member of SWS Group

Dan W. Cook III
Senior Advisor
MHT Partners

Harlan Crow
Chairman
Crow Holdings

Fred Meyer
Chairman
Aladdin Industries, LLC

Henry J. "Bud" Smith
Bud Smith Organization

Thomas W. Smith
Managing Partner
Prescott Investors, Inc.

James C. Thompson, Jr.
Thompson Petroleum Corporation

Jere W. Thompson
President
The Williamsburg Corporation

Michael L. Whalen
President, CEO
Heart of America Restaurants & Inns

Robert J. Wright
President
TWG, Inc.

H. Martin Gibson, Esq.
Patton Boggs LLP
NCPA Corporate Secretary